P[illegible]

Awaken [illegible]

Marsha's wisdom shines through with encouragement as she provides actionable recommendations to help you climb the staircase of spiritual evolution. Her open and non-dogmatic approach will encourage you to tap into your past spiritual path and your inner wisdom, recognizing that each person's journey will be different.
~**Rebecca Whitecotton**, author of *Pull Your Self Together: A True Story of Alternate Realities, Spiritual Healing, and Dimensional Wholeness*

Every now and then, you meet a guide on the ascent that makes your hike a little easier. Marsha is one such guide. The insights and ageless teachings found within these covers will serve as both a trail map and a pillow to rest your head. So, put on your metaphorical hiking boots and start climbing.
~**Brian Luke Seaward, Ph.D.,** Author of *Stand Like Mountain, Flow Like Water: Reflections on Stress and Human Spirituality*

Marsha could talk to a rock, and the rock would be transformed.
~**Marjo Star**, host of Living Out Loud!

Marsha is one of those teachers for the masses. Her bold, courageous, and clear relating of higher spiritual truth minus the dogma has set me free on many levels and has made the process of accessing my soul's guidance simple.
~**Lonnie Nordell**, Spiritual Teacher and Energy Healer

Marsha takes the great teachings of many of humanity's greatest teachers and synthesizes them into an understandable and manageable guide for our own evolution. The nonjudgmental tone allows me to believe that I can become a full living master, too.
~**Lori Rock**, Spiritual Teacher and Facilitator

Having traversed where few in this day and age have gone, Marsha leads the way for others to embrace their true identities.
~**Mary Katherine Frizzell, M.S., LPC**, Holistic Psychologist

Marsha Hankins takes many of the universal truths which may have seemed esoteric or unreachable and brings them into the realm of everyday life through her personal approach and examples from her own experiences. She demonstrates with compassion, understanding, and humility that the spiritual path is not just for the few who travel to the ashram but for everyone here and now in this lifetime. A true master teaches by example, and that is what I see in Marsha's book.
~**Ginger Withee**, Spiritual Teacher and Facilitator

This is a book that I can read over and over, and every time a different level of the truth of Who I Am pops up! What happens when I read this book is that after a few pages, my soul tells me to stop and spend some time in silence integrating what I just read. I can feel the truth of myself as Source.

~**Nadia Mora Lara**, Spiritual Teacher and Facilitator

Awaken to Ascension is a must-read for anyone looking for enlightenment or who wants to be awake. The author's guidance on what it means to prepare for ascension is clearly explained through her own experiences and analogies she has developed to help us understand the process. The book is easy to follow and read, all while passing on fundamental useable knowledge.
~**Debbie Weaver**, Reader

Marsha is one of those rare individuals who excels in having the knowledge *and* the ability to convey it to her readers. She shares her truth, which I have found not to be available just anywhere, in a manner that has allowed me to make significant strides on my journey.
~**Earl Edwards,** Reader

Awaken to Ascension is a valuable resource for anyone earnestly seeking Truth. I found it especially handy as I am a solo sojourner, with few with whom I can compare "notes." Marsha's insights confirmed many I had channeled from Source on my own. Still, others gave me the help I needed to get over a couple of spiritual hurdles that were proving problematic. A great book to keep close for reference, inspiration, and clarification on anyone's journey. Thank you, Marsha!
~**A. Leonard**, Reader

Awaken to Ascension

Mastering Oneness and Knowing Yourself as Source

Marsha Hankins

The author of this book does not dispense medical advice or prescribe the use of any technique as a form of treatment for physical, emotional, or medical problems without the advice of a physician, either directly or indirectly. The intent of the author is only to offer information of a general nature to help you in your quest for emotional and spiritual well-being. In the event you use any of the information in this book for yourself, which is your constitutional right, the author and the publisher assume no responsibility for your actions.

Because of the dynamic nature of the Internet, any web addresses or links contained in this book may have changed since publication and may no longer be valid. The views expressed in this work are solely those of the author and do not necessarily reflect the views of the publisher, and the publisher hereby disclaims any responsibility for them.

Cover by 100 Covers
Graphics by Rebecca Cribelli

ISBN: 978-1-7371279-1-8 (p)
ISBN: 978-1-7371279-0-1 (e)
Library of Congress Control Number: 2022923495

Ascension Now, LLC
Durango, CO
USA

With Love and Gratitude to

The Office of the Christ
For sending so many wonderful teachers
to assist humanity;

My dear friend and mentor,
Kris Duffy,
For loving and supporting me through
my spiritual adolescence;

and
My husband and life partner,
Chip Hankins,
For the many, many lives we have
created together
to get to this stage of our evolution.

Contents

An Invitation

I know you are just beginning this book, but I invite you to do two things at the end.

First, if you find *Awaken to Ascension* helpful to your journey, please recommend it to your friends and rate the book on the site where you purchased it—or on the format of your choice such as Goodreads or Google. Other people want to know what you think, and your feedback is important to me.

Second, I invite you to join my mailing list. As a member, you will receive the free pdf, "7 Steps to Creating Lasting Change in Your Life: A Guide to Personal Transformation," new post notifications for my blog, and announcements about new books and specials. I try to keep it simple.

Join Marsha's Mailing List at https://marshahankins.com/mailing-list/

We are in this process of awakening together. As we go through the steps, our love and support for each other are essential to knowing ourselves as Source. Onward and upward.

Foreword

By Brian Luke Seaward, PhD
Author of *Stand Like Mountain, Flow Like Water: Reflections on Stress and Human Spirituality*

Anyone who has kept his or her fingers on the pulse of the "new age heartbeat" for the past several decades has no doubt heard the term "the ascension process." Despite their familiarity with the term, many people, when asked to elaborate, often come up a bit short. "An expansion of consciousness?" "Jacob's Ladder?" "Enlightenment?" "A trip to Nirvana?" "Died and gone to heaven?" Those people acquainted with the Catholic tradition might offer the first response because any good Catholic knows that the most famous ascension process was achieved by Jesus after the resurrection. There is even a holy day in honor of this event. Catholics (and all other Christians), however, do not have a monopoly on this spiritual process. With a little effort, the ascension process is available to us all.

Consider the act of climbing a mountain. Hikers and bushwhackers alike engage in the ascent of majestic mountains because the view from the top is inviting. From sages and wisdom keepers the world over, the mountain serves as a metaphor for achieving higher consciousness. The clarity from the mountain's summit becomes a metaphor for gaining clarity on our own life's journey. This is why so many people, upon reaching a mountain peak, claim it to be a spiritual experience; they say, "I have kissed the face of God."

Like a mountain with many perspectives from the north, south, east, and west directions, so too does the ascension process have several perspectives and interpretations. And, like a mountain with many paths toward the summit, there are many paths of the ascension process. Perhaps the most commonly cited of these paths from the Eastern tradition is the understanding of the rise of the serpentine spiritual energy from the base of the spine through the chakras through the top of the head (crown chakra). This is what the sages and wisdom keepers from the land of ancient Sanskrit called the rise of the "Kundalini energy." Like any ascent up a mountain top, this rise of sacred spiritual energy is not an easy process. The ascent from the Western tradition, however, is no less challenging.

As far as we know, renowned psychologist Carl G. Jung likely never used the term the ascension process, but he was certainly well aware of it when he described the term "psychic equilibrium." It was Jung's belief that the impediment to higher consciousness was the conscious mind's censor to the wisdom of the unconscious—the ego. To expand one's consciousness, according to Jung, one must become fluent in the languages of the unconscious mind. The unconscious (also called the subconscious) speaks in the language of colors, symbols, metaphors, dream fragments, and archetypes. If we are only using the language skill set of the conscious mind (words and numbers) we are navigating life without a map and compass. Not only will you not ascend, but you will also end up walking in circles. In Jung's words, "Until you make the unconscious conscious, you will see everything in your life as fate." Ironically, taking time to go below the depths of the unconscious mind to explore the inner landscape of this territory is what allows you to rise in consciousness. In the words of Carl Jung, "He who looks outside dreams, he who looks inside awakens."

Expanding consciousness may seem easy. Just open the portals to all of your senses and begin to explore with a curious mind. But what famed mythologist Joseph Campbell referred to as "the call to adventure" is often deafened by the voice of the ego that speaks the language of fear; "Don't go!" Today, many spiritual luminaries speak of the ascension process as more than just an exercise of mental exploration. Rather, expanding consciousness also includes a skill set of emotional intelligence, where one's consciousness shifts from fear to love and compassion. While fear may serve as an important role in the survival from physical danger, it becomes a great liability when it impedes the spiritual journey of the human experiece. Fear, as expressed through the ego's fight-or-flight response, can become the biggest impediment to one's ascension process. Moreover, the walls of protection constructed and reinforced by the ego perpetuate the illusion of separation.

Fear is surely a roadblock on the spiritual path, but it's not the only one to be aware of. At this point in time on planet earth, American culture is one of the great distractions. At no time in previous recorded history have we been bombarded with so much sensory stimulation. The countless portals that have opened up across the digital spectrum now serve as one of the biggest potential roadblocks to higher consciousness. Perhaps as no surprise, the ego plays a role in this process, too. Acquiescing to the fear of missing out (also known as FOMO) of what's going on in the world of social media, video games, binge-watching of screen programming, conspiracy theories, and all other digital enticements will only serve to thwart one's best efforts to go inside and explore the inner landscape. The digital landscape has a glass ceiling. Ascending to the higher realms of consciousness is limitless.

What makes the ascension process so important at this point in time is that humanity is at a crossroads in its evolution where, in order to proceed, we must dissolve the illusion of separation and come to a complete and unfiltered realization that we are in an amazing dance of oneness. We are also about to realize that we are not alone in the cosmos. We are members of a great galactic family of star children, and this realization will only become evident to those who look beyond the veils of illusion to see the vast cosmic tapestry of oneness.

Every now and then, you meet a guide on the ascent that makes your hike a little easier. Marsha is one such guide. The insights and ageless teachings found within these covers will serve as both a trail map and a pillow to rest your head. So, put on your metaphorical hiking boots and start climbing, and above all else, enjoy the view.

[illegible] process [illegible]

[illegible]

[illegible] such a [illegible] for the period [illegible] [illegible] of [illegible] place [illegible] the [illegible] limitless [illegible] the [illegible] of the biggest [illegible]. Perhaps no [illegible] to the fear of [illegible] what [illegible] the world [illegible]

[illegible]

We [illegible] at this [illegible] is [illegible] that humanity is at a crossroads [illegible] dissolve the illusion of separation [illegible] and [illegible] galactic [illegible] children [illegible] the vast [illegible]

Every now and then [illegible]

Preface

The self divides into ten billion distinct illuminating spirits.
Distinguish these without falling into names and classifications.
—Hongzhi

The first edition of this book began in 2013. I had been teaching and writing local articles for many years, and I started getting requests from students and readers to write a book. I had started a book a few years earlier because I was passionate about sharing my spiritual experiences with others, but I had not tried to publish it. When I pulled it off the shelf, I realized that both humanity and I had evolved over the last five years, and I needed to start at the beginning.

When the lightbulb in my head finally turned on to enlighten my sleeping consciousness, I ran full force into my spiritual education. I had many questions that took many years for me to answer. To start this book, I made a list of the questions I often got in classes and the topics people wanted me to discuss in more detail. When I organized the list, I had the outline for my book. I expanded a few topics and clarified some areas where readers had questions. I was excited about the first edition of this book, *Ascension: The End of Duality*. But, because our frequency continues to go higher, I was guided to create an updated version.

Awaken to Ascension: Mastering Oneness and Knowing Yourself as Source is about achieving spiritual mastery. We all have many questions. If we are serious about learning, we keep asking until we find our answers. We also learn that we have many levels of understanding to move through to graduate from our time on Earth and our experiences as human beings.

My classes have always drawn both those who consider themselves spiritual beginners and long-time students looking for clarity on what felt to them like advanced concepts. Yet, in this mixed group of people, everyone would get what they needed from the same class. I believe the same is true for this book. We always have something to learn, and we will find what we need when we set our intentions and then pay attention. Sometimes we find our answers in unexpected places.

You may feel lost and forgotten, but you are not. You only have temporary amnesia. Now is the time to wake up completely and embrace your journey to the full remembrance of yourself as Source, as the creator, as the master that you are.

I have included definitions in the introduction that explain how I use certain spiritual terms. All practices do not use the same definitions for some words, and words may have different meanings at different levels of consciousness. These differences have often confused some of my students in classes, so I am giving these definitions upfront to be sure that you understand what I am discussing versus what you might have learned in another process. Rigid definitions of terms are not important. However, a platform for a clear understanding of the principles and energy is essential.

I hope this book is the spiritual roadmap that will help you take your next steps on your journey to spiritual mastery. Reviewing it has reminded me of how far I have come *and* the many steps I still have ahead.

With Love,

Marsha

Chapter 1

An Introduction

Never believe that you live by the power of food
and not by the power of God!
—Sri Yukteswar, *Autobiography of a Yogi* by Paramahansa Yogananda

Remembering who we are as Source is an exciting journey. It can also be confusing and a little scary at times. As we recognize ourselves as spiritual beings, we change our lives. Some of those changes are easy, but others are not. Understanding how we got here (and why) helps us release judgment and fear. Understanding where we are going and how to get there makes the changes easier to integrate.

Our spiritual evolution is very personal. We read books, take classes, and go to religious services to learn more about our spiritual nature and truth. However, the choice to move forward is ours, and only ours. As we say, it is always an inside job.

I have experienced the full range of human emotions connected to awakening to my spiritual truth. Not only is the journey a roller coaster ride, but it is also often a process of two steps forward and one step back. When we experience an expansion of spiritual energy, the joy can be almost overwhelming, but so can the fear of greater spiritual awareness and the power that comes with it. I am sharing parts of my journey in this book, but most importantly, I am sharing things I have learned that I hope will help you on your road to ascension.

The language I use in this book is for western man. I cherish my background in eastern philosophies and techniques, but I know that many westerners are confused and burdened by the ancient esoteric texts, Sanskrit terms, and eastern practices. I take a contemporary approach that has served my students and me well. I hope it will serve you, too.

****

From many years of studying, teaching, and talking with people from around the world, I have learned that Ascension means different things to different people. While it would seem that spiritual students and metaphysicians would speak the same language, we do not. The different traditions and the various spiritual and religious philosophies may use the same words, but those words do not always mean the same things.

When I began my spiritual journey in earnest, I did not know what I truly believed. I certainly did not understand the language. I had to learn to translate terminology and practices from one program to another as I wandered through the maze of spiritual possibilities that came my way. Eventually, I found what was right for me, but that was only the beginning. I had much to learn and still do because our spiritual evolution is an ever-continuing road.

I was not born tuned into my psychic abilities. I did not see auras, talk to angels, or have premonitions about the future when I was young. I was just an average kid growing up in a Christian household with many unanswered questions.

While I had a small interest in spiritually-based reading as I grew up and studied Transcendental Meditation in my thirties, I did not begin a serious exploration of my spiritual self until well into my forties. Little did I know that all the questions I had as a child would come back to me and that I would finally find my answers.

The road to this point in my life and evolution has been fascinating to me. Looking back at who I was earlier in my life and who I am now, I feel as though I am looking at two different people. In many ways, I am two different people. That is how it should be for all of us if we are evolving in any way. Who we were in the past is not who we are now, and who we are now is not who we will be in the future. We are not designed to remain the same throughout our lives.

Our evolution is to remember who we are as spiritual beings. We came from the light, but our memories inside what is known as the Experiment in Duality got a bit foggy. While we seem to have been lost in that fog for a long time, we simply have to be ready to sweep away the distractions and remember our divine truth. The good news is that this process has never been as easy as it is now. Humanity is waking up very quickly, and many are stepping forward today to share their stories and their techniques for finding joy and achieving divine oneness. This book is about mine.

When I finally began a serious exploration of my spiritual self, I had no real concept of where it would lead. I knew that I was looking for a way to connect with what I believed was "beyond," but I wasn't sure what that meant either. I just knew there was more.

I never expected to find myself teaching others how to become spiritual masters. I was a dancer, an accountant, a salesperson, a tutor, a corporate wife, and more, but not a spiritual guide or teacher. However, the possibilities are unlimited once we open to our true nature instead of what society tries to program us to be. We each have natural skills, talents, and passions that we brought into this world. We simply need to allow ourselves to discover what we came here to do. That is what happened for me when I surrendered.

Religion Begins

The first thing I had to surrender was my attachment to what I thought religion meant, especially my parents' chosen religion of Christianity. Today's spiritual student is continually trying to sort through religion versus spirituality.

What we call *religion* began with a set of foundational principles based on the teachings of a spiritual leader. That leader may have had a very high frequency and, therefore, put forward a high-frequency set of principles. In other cases, the frequency of the leader was not so high. In either case, these masters never set out to create religions. They only desired to share what they knew to be their spiritual truth.

It is difficult for many to see that Jesus did not create Christianity, and Buddha did not create Buddhism. These religions, like others, were created by the followers of the great masters who could not fully grasp what they were being told—that everyone is an aspect of Source and has that power within. Because they could not fully understand, these followers created stories, processes, and structures around what they believed their masters were saying, and religions were born.

The Gospel of Matthew tells this story of Jesus' baptism: "And when Jesus had been baptized, just as he came up from the water, suddenly the heavens were opened to him and he saw the Spirit of God descending like a dove and alighting on him. And a voice from heaven said, 'This is my Son, the Beloved, with whom I am well pleased.' "[1]

The traditional reader of *The Bible* does not recognize that this is the experience for all who awaken to the full presence and power of the Christ within. Jesus' teachings were replete with messages of our divinity and our place in the Divine Kingdom. He taught that the kingdom of the Father was within each of us. He taught that anything he could do, we could do, and even greater things. How did this get lost from what is now the mainstream religion of Christianity?

I believe everyone would benefit from an honest, in-depth study of their chosen religion. It is not always easy, but it is doable. I speak mainly about Christianity because that is my background. I know, however, from my readings and from conversations with others who have done what I have, that the history of every religion is rarely fully known or revealed to its followers.

I truly honor and respect each of the great religions of humankind. They have each brought us significant divine truth in an attempt to bring humanity closer to the Creator. However, as the great line from the song in

---

[1] Matthew 3:16-17, *NRSV Bible with the Apocrypha*, Kindle Edition, HarperCollins, New York, NY, 2011.

the musical *Porgy and Bess* says, "The t'ings dat yo' li'ble to read in de Bible, it ain't necessarily so."[2]

Religion Cycles

I did not come to recognize that I had always understood the Christ in a way that my parents and the church would not have been able to understand until I began to explore my spirituality as an adult. I have always felt a connection to the Christ that does not fit into the Christian religion. However, it does fit what I believe to be true Christianity, the original teachings of Master Jesus, and the experience of the early Christians who knew a level of oneness and equality with the Christ that I did not find in the modern Christian teachings.

The history of every religion seems to be one of many cycles. The original teacher puts forth teachings that later become institutionalized and dogmatized, with strict rules and procedures imposed on the followers. When the principles get too far off track, a new teacher arrives to try to put the train back on track. This course correction may last awhile, but sooner or later, the train begins to derail, and another leader arrives to try to set things straight.

I am not a religious historian and will not pretend to be. I know what I have studied, what my self-as-Source tells me is true, and what I have come to believe. No matter what I share, I encourage everyone to be seriously interested in doing research and coming to their conclusions. There are unlimited resources available.

A brief history of the Judeo-Christian tradition begins with the king and high priest, Lord Melchizedek. Melchizedek taught the founding principles of spirituality on earth at the very early stages of our evolution. His teaching became the foundation of the Kabala and many of the early mystery schools. Melchizedek taught the connection between humanity and Source and reminded human beings that they were not separate from God.

As the Jewish tradition moved through time, these teachings became distorted. When Judea divided into various tribes, the Levitical Order

[2] Gershwin, George and Ira, "It Ain't Necessarily So," *Porgy and Bess*, 1935.

acquired the power of religious leadership and separated the people from God. Followers were to go to the rabbis versus having a direct connection to the Father.

King David arrived and gave the power back to his people by reinstating Melchizedek's principles as best he could. Over time, the principles and teachings of much of the Jewish tradition drifted off track again. Master Jesus graced this planet with his presence and teachings to remind people who they were.

The story is the same for Buddha and his quest for spiritual truth. At the time of Buddha's birth, Hindu practices had degraded to the worship of the various gods and goddesses that were originally teachers for the follower of this ancient practice. The teachings of Krishna and other great gurus had become lost to many Hindus. Buddha went in search of a great master to help him find his way. When he could not find the one he sought, he went within and discovered his way to enlightenment, which later became Buddhism. In time, other great masters arrived to put Hinduism back on its original path.

Constantine Changed Everything

The most significant shift in the course of what is known as Christianity came during the rule of Roman Emperor Constantine. The Roman Empire had a growing number of followers of Jesus, who had taught them that they were of God and had the power of God. Who needs an emperor when you have the power of God?

In 314 A.D., Constantine decided to take control. He announced that God had come to him and directed him to rewrite sections of *The Bible* and church doctrine, under God's guidance, of course. Over the next thirty years, Christianity was remade in "Constantine's image" as he sought to create a church that would placate the followers of Jesus but give the Emperor the power.

Constantine instituted the concept that Jesus was the one and only Son of God. He removed the teaching of reincarnation and created the story of Mary Magdalen as a prostitute. The list goes on and on.

Letters of protest from bishops down to priests poured into Rome. They asked, what gave Constantine the power to rewrite church doctrine and change the teachings of the Christ? The answer was, essentially, follow me, go to prison, or leave the church. One did not mess with the Roman Emperor.

Many did leave the church. The Gnostics, the Arians, and other groups chose to hold on to their beliefs and go their own way. These groups were labeled heretics, a stigma I have heard taught by the church even today.

Changes in *The Bible* and the doctrine of Christianity have continued since the time of Constantine. Why is any of this important? Because we need to understand what we believe and why we believe it, whether institutionalized religion, New Age, atheism, or other spiritual philosophy.

One of the most interesting points of the intervention into Christianity by Constantine was that he was not a follower of the Christ or a church member. He was not baptized as a Christian until after he had molded the religion to his liking. He was reported to have ridiculed the followers of Jesus by calling them *christis*, or "little christs." And yet, he became the "father" of Christianity as it has been taught for hundreds of years, even though most Christians do not know the history.

As I will continue to say, I have always felt my strong connection to Master Jesus and what, for me, is true Christianity. I honor the followers of the Christian church and the followers of Buddhism, Hinduism, Judaism, New Age, and more. We each need to find our way to our truth. Understanding the origins of various teachings and why we believe what we think we believe is essential to knowing that truth and standing in our power as sovereign aspects of Source.

My Understanding, My Truth

Eventually, I came to understand what my intuition had always been trying to tell me—I knew more on the inner than I was taught on the outer. As I explored my thoughts and feelings and broadened my scope of reading, I realized that who I am in this life is New Age. New Age encompasses all the great spiritual teachings from the beginning of time in a format that makes sense to me. All New Age teachings are not the same, but this is the best category for me if we need labels.

I have been able to find a home for everything I thought was my truth under the umbrella of "New Age" and "New Thought." For example, I intuitively believed in reincarnation from the beginning of this life. My personal experiences have made it very real for me. For those who are still wondering if other lives can be real, I recommend the works of Dr. Ian Stevenson and Dr. Jim Tucker, who have documented the past life memories of thousands of children who said they had been someone else before.

The overall most important point of enlightenment for me was learning that Christ is a spiritual office held by many masters over the years, not just the role of Master Jesus. The teachings of the Office of the Christ through Melchizedek, Jesus, and others transcend all religions and encompass all the aspects of christ consciousness. Understanding the Christ as a position in the Spiritual Hierarchy and christ consciousness as part of our DNA allowed me to open myself fully to the ancient teachings in a way I had not allowed previously. I was on a new path.

I was guided to Kris Duffy and the I Am Source™ program in December 1999. The teachings of this program became my foundation for Ascension. I began teaching and facilitating I Am Source™ in 2000 and still follow its principles today because they still make more sense to me than anything else I have studied, ancient or New Age.

After Kris transitioned from this planet in 2009, her parents asked me to continue her work and take the program wherever I thought it should go. Through channeling to the Christ and my self-as-Source, new classes and techniques were added until a new series, Standing in the Light®, emerged in 2010. There are still many new and exciting things to learn and many directions my road may take. As I pursue my evolution, I have retired from teaching Standing in the Light® and passed its course to the brilliant teachers of the program who will continue to expand it in service to the Source and humanity.

What I share in this book is a combination of what I have learned from my personal experiences as a teacher, a healer, and an ever-growing spiritual being. Most importantly, I share what I have learned from my self-as-Source—the divine within me. I accept nothing as my truth at this level of my being without testing it through my soul. No one should. The ability to channel clearly to one's guidance and trust one's intuition is of utmost importance on the road to Ascension. What works for one may not work for others.

What Are We Doing Here?

As spiritual beings, we are always seeking ways to expand our love, wisdom, and creative power. The continuous seeking for expansion leads to the choice to experience ourselves in many forms on many planets or stars to continue our spiritual growth. For some of us, the journey of spiritual evolution brought us to planet earth and the Experiment in Duality—what St. Germain and others have called the Great Experiment.

Duality is not our truth. The Experiment in Duality is just that—an experiment in the duality of wills. Before this "experiment," we knew ourselves only as one. To understand more about ourselves as one, we created a plan to experience the opposite of being one. As the Native Americans say, walk a hundred miles in my moccasins if you want to understand my life. That is what we decided to do.

While the purpose of this plan has been explained through teachings from the Archangels and the Ascended Masters, I have found that very few people truly understand it. Once I finally got it, everything shifted for me. I moved from judgment of the experiences on earth to acceptance and appreciation. My entire healing process accelerated because I found it easier to let go. What did I come to understand and accept?

I came to understand and accept that we chose to experience ourselves as separate from each other and Source for a purpose. The intention was to expand our understanding of love and oneness by understanding what it was like to be without love and oneness. The plan was never to be dark or evil or to create pain or suffering. It was always about growth through new experiences.

While the experiment began very smoothly, we lost control, and we are just now finding our way out; but we are finding our way out quickly. As we continue to release our remaining judgments and accept what we have learned, we are breaking down the old paradigm to create space for the new.

The transition from old to new, from separation to oneness, is why things in the outer world look so chaotic at this time.

We Are All on the Road to Ascension

Ascension is viewed by many as the way to get off the planet. They seek a way to get out of what they perceive to be a mess, but that is not the goal. The goal is to bring back the experience of divine oneness with All That Is—to know unconditional love for All That Is. Only when that is achieved for each of us will we be ready to end duality and ascend from this planet.

The ascension process has been very challenging on earth because we have been in the midst of the experiment. The density of the experiment is not the normal state for children of Source, and we have found it difficult to remember who we are. However, we are remembering, and everyone is going home.

I once had a student ask me how she could help her husband get onto his spiritual path. I asked, "What makes you believe he is not?" She immediately understood what I was saying. Since our first incarnation on earth, we have been evolving. Every lesson learned has taken us one step closer to the end of duality. Where anyone is now is simply a function of what they packed in their "spiritual suitcase" for this lifetime and where they are in the "conga line."

The terms "young soul" and "old soul" are commonly used in spiritual and metaphysical circles. I find looking at this concept as either "new to the planet" or "old to the planet" to be a better perspective. The people at the end of the conga line (those who came most recently) have not had as much time to learn and evolve as those at the head of the conga line who came here first. It is not a matter of good or bad. It is merely a matter of recognizing and accepting through which stage of evolution someone is moving. Patience, understanding, compassion, and forgiveness are essential on this journey.

Sharing What I Have Learned

I love teaching. I love working one-on-one with people who truly want to find their way. I love sharing with others what has helped me reach this point in my life, which is the purpose of this book.

When I was first guided to write a book on Ascension and moving into oneness, I was not sure what I would say. This topic can be approached in many ways. I have been guided to share the process that we are going through as we shift from where we are in our human form back into ourselves as pure light. While I will share some techniques and suggestions for ascension, this book is about understanding the energetics of how we got here and how we will get out. It is about understanding what we did to create the density of human form and reversing that process to come out of the experiment. It is about knowing that there is light at the end of the tunnel, even though we may have rough days.

That does not mean that the how-tos are not important. They are. There are many how-tos from which to choose. I am very fond of the saying that there are many roads to the Buddha. There is no one path home to our light. However, no matter which path we choose, we are all going through the same energetic process of moving from our density into our light. Understanding the process made it much easier for me to surrender to what my soul guided me to do. Understanding that process also made it easier for me to accept that so many different roads can lead to the same destination—Ascension.

The road to Ascension is not an outer world journey but an inner world one. The journey is not about how things look on the outer. The outer world is an illusion. The journey is about how things feel on the inner. The journey is about self-exploration—peeling away the layers of false beliefs and false realities to find divine truth and rediscover ourselves as Source.

A process is required. We do not wake up one day fully enlightened and ready to ascend from the experiment. When we do wake up to who we are as spiritual beings, we must each find a process for spiritual evolution that works for us. Whatever that process is, it must be balanced.

We all need a combination of meditation, learning, and a vision for service to achieve the full spiritual realization of ourselves as Source in human form. One path is not enough to understand and experience all that we need to achieve oneness.

For example, the Hindus teach that there are three primary paths to Ascension: the path of Devotion (meditation), the path of Wisdom (knowledge), and the path of Selfless Service (being of service). However, no matter which primary path a student feels is right for them, all of these elements must be included to achieve spiritual balance and oneness with the divine.

I did not come across this Hindu teaching until I was well into my spiritual journey. When I did, I immediately recognized that my primary path was wisdom. For years, I had actively studied various approaches to spirituality, but more importantly, I had channeled notebooks full of information on topics about healing energy and the ascension process.

I was also graced with wonderful teachers along the way who taught me the importance of balance. Nothing is more important than what we learn from our self-as-Source. We are Source in physical form. All the answers *do* lie inside, but until our frequency is high enough to access all that information, we need teachers to help us find our way. Even after we can clearly channel our guidance, we need help from time to time to get past the resistance of the lower-self who still buys into the illusion.

Duality Is an Illusion

An illusion is something that deceives by producing a false or misleading impression of reality.[3] The experiment created the illusion of duality, the illusion of separation from Source. We have always been one. We will always be one. Anything that tells us differently is part of the illusion.

Breaking free is simple. Just wake up and stop buying into separation. However, just because something is simple does not mean it is easy. Hopefully, the pages that follow will give you an understanding of why it has

---

[3] *Random House Webster's College Dictionary*, Random House, Inc., New York, NY, 1991.

been so challenging and what you can do to make it easier to break free of the illusion.

Remember that we are designed to do this. We came here with a plan to learn and a plan to get out. The Experiment in Duality is not permanent. It is not real. Each of us must accept that for ourselves and choose to leave it behind. No one is on this journey alone, but the final choice to let go can only be ours. It is time to shatter the illusion and remember ourselves as one.

Understanding Terminology

We have limited language in the West to describe a variety of approaches to our spirituality. However, it is important to know what we are talking about so that we have a common ground for understanding and know if we are comparing apples to apples instead of apples to oranges.

Therefore, I am including some definitions in the introduction and explaining how I use these terms. I am not attached to how we use words, just that we understand each other. The first big one, of course, is *God.* What is the difference between God, Goddess, and Source?

Who or What Is "God?"

Many people have problems using the word God. They understandably view this term through the narrow definitions of various religions that do not speak to their spiritual needs. I do not have issues using the words God or Goddess because I see them as aspects or versions of Source—the energetic source of all creation.

The word originally translated into God was a non-gendered term for the creator. In ancient languages, the words that became God most often meant the One, the Great Unity, or the Source. However, considering the dogma that religions have put onto the name God, it is no wonder people have difficulty deciding who or what God is or deciding what to call the greater part of themselves. The challenge for many people is to embrace the concept of a source of creation without religious restrictions until they can decide for themselves who or what God, or the source, is to them.

Like any other word, *god* has many definitions in the dictionary: a superhuman being, a supreme leader, the creator, or a religious figure. It is used in upper or lower case depending on its meaning. Today, the concept of God ranges from the multiple gods (and goddesses) of Hinduism to the traditional Christian, Jewish, and Islamic God outside of ourselves to the inner God of New Age and New Thought to whatever one believes God may be.

Many versions of God, or Source, can lead to Ascension, not just one. Hindus include many gods in their philosophy to represent the many aspects of the divine. Buddhists do not believe in God because they see God as a being outside of oneself and, therefore, disempowering. Yet, both of these blessed traditions have given this planet many ascended masters. Christians who understand the original teachings of Jesus instead of the myth created under the rule of Constantine know that Ascension can also be attained through the teachings of Jesus.

The definitions I give below are important for conveying specific concepts and maintaining a common language for exploration. My only goal is sharing concepts, not creating more dogma.

Source: the original energy and intelligence of all creation.

- Everything exists inside "the body of Source." As Source creates, Source expands.
- Nothing physical or etheric can be separate from Source. Source is All That Is.

The God/Goddess: the spiritual representatives of the male and female creative components of Source.

- The Goddess, the feminine energy, is the receiving component of creation. She is the space in which ideas and intentions form. Nothing begins without a vision.

- God, the masculine energy, is the active component of creation. He is the energy moving through the intention to bring it into form. Nothing is created without some form of movement.
- One component cannot create without the other. The God/Goddess is a beautiful and essential collaboration.
- I use the term God/Goddess instead of Source when I need to emphasize the male/female energy of creation.
- I use God or Goddess when appropriate to the male or female energy specifically.

The God/Goddess/All That Is: the extension of the God/Goddess as creative energy to encompass all creation.

- Everything exists inside the body of Source. However, the expression "God/Goddess/All That Is" means all parts of creation and honors the male and female energies that created it.

The Spiritual Hierarchy: the structure of the governing body of the universe.

- The universe is an organization of energy, both physical and metaphysical.
- Every organization needs a hierarchy of responsibility to keep it operating as effectively as possible.
- The members of the Spiritual Hierarchy are beings of higher frequencies with specific areas of expertise and experience. They range from teachers to planners to creators.
- Their job is to advise and guide the evolution of the universe. They are here to assist us, not to command us. They can be called on for help, but they are not our source.

Who or what is the Christ?

Another challenge for many people is letting go of the current Christian Church version of the Christ. The Christ is an office in the Spiritual Hierarchy. While Master Jesus was a physical representation of the Christ on Earth, he was not the only one we have known.

- The role of the Office of the Christ is teacher and guide for the Divine Plan for the ascension of humanity.
- The office transcends all religions and spiritual philosophies. The Christ is neither male nor female, but both.
- Because the Christ is an office and not a proper noun, I refer to "the Christ" versus Christ as we refer to "the President" versus President Lincoln.
- Because the English language does not contain an appropriate androgynous pronoun (*it* just does not work), I am guided to follow tradition and refer to the Christ as male.

Other Definitions for Common Ground

I am giving a brief overview of other common terms used in spiritual circles that may not always mean the same thing. Some people have tried to create a standard dictionary of spiritual terminology, but that is not practical or necessary. We just need to listen to each other and be flexible. The following definitions apply to the rest of my writing.

The self-as-Source, the soul, the god-self: the highest individualized aspect of ourselves as Source.

- Many practices use the word *soul* to define a lower aspect of our energy structure, while others put the *soul* at the top of the energy structure.
- In various practices, the soul can mean the small essence of Source held in the human body, the higher-self, the god-self, the self-as-Source, or the soul. All these definitions work as long as one understands how the word *soul* is used.
- Through this book, I will use the terms soul and self-as-Source interchangeably.

The lower-self: the aspect of ourselves that believes it is human—the physical, emotional, and mental bodies.

- The lower-self is concerned with its physical safety, emotional comfort, and 3rd-dimensional belief systems and values.
- The lower-self is the aspect that needs healing. It is the part of us that believes it has been separate from Source and needs to remember who it is.
- The lower-self is also referred to as the ego-self, the base-self, the personality-self, the little-self, etc. in other practices.
- In my practice, I refer to the *ego* as the unique reflection of who we are as Source. Under this definition, we have a level of ego at each dimension of who we are. The ego at the lower-self level is not inadequate or inferior. It does not remember that it is divine, and that is all.

Frequency: the rate at which energy moves.

- Our frequency determines how we feel at any moment and is an indication of our overall spiritual progress.
- A slow rate of movement is what we call low frequency and feels denser or darker.
- A fast rate of movement is what we call high frequency and feels lighter or brighter.
- Each person has a personal frequency for where they are in their evolution. As one's frequency goes higher, the level of one's consciousness goes higher.

The conga line: the chain of human frequencies in which we exist from the most spiritually evolved master leading the way to the densest being who is anchoring the end of the line.

- We did not all come to this planet at the same time. Those who came first are generally toward the front of the conga line. As others chose to enter this experiment, they added themselves to the back of the line.
- One's place in line is not determined solely by how long one has been inside the experiment. We each have the opportunity to make

choices each day that determine the rate at which we move out of our darkness.
- There is no judgment on one's place in the conga line. We each came with our plan for what we wanted to experience and learn. One path is not better than another, and all positions in line are sacred.

Spiritual suitcase: the issues, gifts, and talents we choose to explore in each life.
- As we set our agendas for each incarnation, we decide what issues we want to work toward healing and what gifts and talents we want to share with the world.
- What we "pack in our spiritual suitcases" will determine the events and situations we attract into our lives and the experiences that we need to go through to achieve what we came to learn.

Guidance: the voice of Source within.
- The "inner voice" that comes from our self-as-Source has all the wisdom and knowledge of the universe. This voice has the answers to all that we need.
- What is in our highest good cannot always be known by the lower-self. The knowingness of our highest good needs to come from our soul. Otherwise, we are giving our power to others.

Channeling: the ability to connect to and receive information from other realms.
- A psychic channel is an open line of communication, like a radio or television channel.
- Everyone can learn and master this skill with the right technique and practice.
- The critical question is, how open and how clear is the channel?
- Getting clear guidance depends on one's ability to be a clear channel. One can "channel" to one's lower-self, which means one hears what one wants to hear versus what one needs to hear. This distinction is essential when trying to follow the highest plan.

The Divine Plan: the highest frequency plan for the evolution of the universe.

- The God/Goddess has a general plan for the progress of creation.
- Our souls, our selves-as-Source, know the Divine Plan for each of us individually and how that plan integrates into the Divine Plan for all.
- The details of the plan must fluctuate based on the choices and outcomes related to a wide variety of events.
- Getting clear guidance and holding the space for change are essential to being in alignment with the plan.

The Experiment in Duality (or the Great Experiment): an experiment in the energies of the perception of separation.

- An experiment is a process for discovering something unknown or testing a principle or procedure.
- The Experiment in Duality is the opportunity to learn from the experience of being in opposition to Divine Will (the highest good of all) instead of being in alignment with divine oneness.
- It has expanded our knowledge of love and oneness through the experience of ourselves as separate beings instead of ourselves as part of a whole.
- The experiment is being conducted in multiple galaxies of our universe, not just on Earth.

Awakening: the moment one becomes genuinely aware of oneself as a spiritual being.

- Awakening goes beyond the intellectual concept that we are spiritual beings to the experience of knowing this without question.
- Individual awakenings may take many forms, but the outcome is the same—one fully understands that we are all more than this physical experience.

Clearing: raising the frequency surrounding an issue such that it is resolved or healed.

- The term clearing is used in metaphysical circles for "clearing away" whatever energies cause us to remain in lower-frequency behaviors or situations.
- Any technique that takes our frequency higher is a form of clearing.
- Clearing away old energies to make way for new, higher-frequency energies is the key to evolution and ascension.

Ascension: moving higher in frequency.

- Ascension with a small *a* is the process of raising our frequency one step at a time. In this respect, we have always been and will always be ascending.
- Ascension with a capital *A* is the point when our frequency rises so high that the next steps in our evolution must be taken beyond our physical forms. Ascension with a capital *A* is our graduation from the earthly plane to the next realm.

Special Considerations

Those who write about spirituality and metaphysics are challenged when trying to fit 5th-dimensional concepts into a 3rd-dimensional format. To those people who seek to maintain the best in American grammar, please bear with me as I break a few rules.

Understanding three techniques I use that might not follow our traditional rules of grammar will be helpful before reading the rest of this book. I have been guided to use these three techniques to emphasize the difference between the ways some concepts are viewed in 3rd-dimensional consciousness versus how they are viewed in 5th-dimensional consciousness. Our ability to shift our consciousness is dependent on our willingness to move our perspective from our 3rd-dimensional selves to our 5th-dimensional selves. I know from my own experience that this is not always easy to do. I am using the following techniques from this point forward.

The first challenge was identifying what are proper nouns in the upper realms but might not necessarily be considered so in traditional grammar. For example, we have the concept of a god/goddess. We also have the beings that hold the offices of the God/Goddess. Because we do not have names for these beings, we use the title God/Goddess. While we know a being to be an ascended master, he or she is a member of the Ascended Masters. I have been guided to honor what I understand to be proper nouns, such as the God/Goddess, Source, the Divine Plan, and others, that might otherwise be written in lowercase.

The second challenge was whether the God/Goddess is singular or plural. It is both. God and Goddess are two separate offices and beings with different energies. However, they are also one unit of creation. I have been guided to use the God/Goddess as a plural term to reflect both the male and female aspects of who they are as that unit.

The third challenge was how to identify lower and higher frequencies of the same words. Many words have one meaning at a lower frequency but a different meaning at a higher frequency. I have already explained the difference between *ascension* and *Ascension*. We also have human emotions, such as love, compassion, and forgiveness, which are very different from the divine feeling states of divine love, divine compassion, and divine forgiveness. Emotions are knee-jerk reactions inside the 3rd-dimensional paradigm. Divine feeling states transcend those emotions to take us into divine oneness with our selves-as-Source.

For example, forgiveness at the 3rd dimensional level of consciousness comes with conditions: I will forgive you when you do so and so. In the divine realms, forgiveness is unconditional. Everything we have experienced in the experiment of separation must be transcended. Ascension is about raising our frequencies so that we no longer experience the lower frequency emotions of our human selves but only experience the higher frequency states of our selves-as-Source. I discuss this in more detail in Chapter 8.

In my community, we use lowercase for emotions and uppercase for the higher frequency states of being. However, that can be confusing, and the constant use of *divine* can be tedious. I am following the current publishing guidelines to eliminate as many capitalized words as possible. When Source wants to emphasize the higher frequency feeling states of the soul over the lower frequency emotions of the lower-self, I use *divine* for that emphasis.

I know that not capitalizing words traditionally capitalized in spiritual writing seems odd to many readers, but we can handle change. I am still capitalizing what I hold to be proper nouns, such as Source, the Divine Plan, and All That Is.

Finding One's Truth

I wrote this book to share what has helped me on my journey in hopes that it will also help you. In the classroom, I ask students to hold open the possibility that what I have to say may be true. We must all decide what works and what does not work for us, what we believe and what we do not believe. Self-discovery is part of the journey out of the Experiment in Duality. We will not all take the same road to Ascension, but we will all arrive at the same place—the full remembrance of ourselves as Source in human form.

I have structured this book as a series of classes. Each chapter covers one component or concept important to the ascension process, and each could easily be expanded into an entire book on its own. I have covered the key elements of each topic and left more for each person to explore. Finally, each chapter lays the energetic foundation for the next chapter, which means the frequency continues to increase throughout the book. As I do in class, I have included parts of my journey and some stories shared by students in my classes. I hope you gain insights that take you deeper into your truth, help you clarify where you are on your journey, and fill your process of ascension with great joy.

Chapter 2

The Road to Here

For no one lights a lamp and puts it under a basket, nor does one put it in a hidden place. Rather, one puts it on a stand that all who come and go will see its light.
—*The Gospel of Thomas,* verse 33, as translated by Marvin Meyer

We each have our story. My road to this stage of my evolution is probably not that exciting to anyone but me, but the road I have traveled and how I got to here is important. I am most grateful to the people who have shared their stories of spontaneous awakening and dramatic journeys into their spiritual enlightenment. Those stories kept me going whenever I began to question whether I was going crazy or just waking up to who I am as Source. However, most people wake up and move into the experience of their light one small, medium, or large step at a time in a way that seems uneventful to others but has a powerful impact on who they are and how they find their way home to their light.

We have been on a journey of spiritual evolution from the moment we were each created as a unique aspect of Source. Everything in physical creation has a cycle of birth, growth, decline, and death. That is because the physical world is limited, and one thing must end for another to begin. The spiritual realm, however, is endless. As the spiritual beings that we are, our growth and evolution are eternal. We never die. We continue to expand.

The part of us that exists beyond our physical form is our true self. Many metaphors have been used to explain how we got here and how we can exist in both physical and spiritual forms. It is said that we are spiritual beings having a human (or earthly) experience. As human beings, we often see ourselves as small and insignificant. As spiritual beings, we know ourselves as unlimited and are always looking for ways to expand ourselves as part of Source.

Like everyone on the planet, I volunteered to be here as part of the Experiment in Duality. It took quite a few years for me to understand and accept that I was not a victim of this earthly creation but came by choice as an empowered creator. The concept that what we have been through on earth is part of a divine experiment in which we chose to participate is not always well received. However, this teaching has been given to us many times by many great masters. Once I understood and accepted the purpose of this experiment, the road to the remembrance of who I am became easier and more joyful. I have come to appreciate the gift of this experience and am grateful for my choice to play this game.

Of course, I did not always feel that way. I have kicked and screamed on my road to oneness and Ascension as many times as I have sung and danced. Most of the journey has been expansive and exciting, but everyone has to face their demons, and I am no different. While we might intellectually understand that we are light and love and blessed children of Source, we must move through many levels of dogma, subconscious beliefs, and programmed behaviors to fully accept ourselves as the beings of light and love that we are. We have to clear away the layers of lack of forgiveness for what we perceive we have done wrong to know the truth of ourselves as Source in our hearts. Then, we can end the duality of the experiment and ascend into pure light. While we have always been light and love, and can only be light and love, we have been buried in the darkness of this experience for a very long time and need to allow ourselves the patience to come back into our selves-as-Source. It is time to let go.

We created an intricate and fascinating experiment in separation throughout this universe. An *experiment* is a test, a trial, or a tentative procedure, especially one for discovering something unknown or testing a principle or procedure.[4] I will explain my understanding of the Experiment in Duality and why we chose to experience separation later. However, I will say now that we did a bang-up job of pushing the experiment to its limits. We have gone as far as we can into the experience of separation, and all we have to do now is come back out. Coming out can be as simple and easy as we allow it to be through our trust and surrender.

Do we have to surrender and come out? No, but I highly recommend it! The love and joy on the other side are too good to pass up.

My Beginnings

When I seriously began my spiritual journey, I thought I already knew almost everything. I had read a few books and done a little meditation. How much more could there be? A few more classes and a bit more practice, and surely I would arrive at mastery. Every time I learned something new, I thought I was almost there. All of this was so exciting. I just could not understand why everyone didn't get it, and I wanted to share my vast knowledge and enthusiasm with the world. I did not yet understand the journey from spiritual infancy to spiritual adolescence to spiritual maturity.

One of my favorite Eastern sayings relative to our spiritual studies is that the further we go, the more we know we have to learn. We all wake up to our spiritual mastery in time. However, we are merely spiritual infants when we first awaken. We have so much to learn and must go through all the stages of growing up (just like human children) to understand and know ourselves as masters. The road is a fascinating and oh-so-rewarding one. However, it requires patience and fortitude to slog through our issues to get back to our light.

As I said and will say again, we have always been light, but our memories inside the experiment become foggy. We simply have to sweep away the distractions so that we can remember. The good news is that this process has never been as easy as it is now. The increased frequency of Mother Earth and humanity makes it possible to make quantum leaps in evolution

---

[4] *Random House Webster's College Dictionary*, Random House, Inc., New York, NY, 1991.

when we choose to do so. We only need to pick a process that works for us and follow it to the remembrance of ourselves as aspects of Source and find our readiness for Ascension.

There are, as the saying goes, many roads to the Buddha. Jesus said, "My Father's mansion has many rooms." Lord Krishna taught, "Any path you travel, I will be there." It took a while for me to find my road in this life. My dedicated study began with the I Am Source™ program, where I was introduced to the concept of the Office of the Christ.

The Christ has been both embraced and rejected, primarily because we have not been taught who or what the Christ is. The Christ is an office in the Spiritual Hierarchy that has been held by many great masters, including Lord Maitreya, Lord Kuthumi, and Master Jesus. The role of the Office of the Christ is to assist humanity in understanding the Experiment in Duality and the Divine Plan for ending it. All who have held the office in a physical body or in the higher realms are great teachers sent to us by Source for our ascension into Ascension.

The first embodied aspect of the Christ on earth was the king and high priest, Lord Melchizedek. The teachings given to us by Melchizedek became the foundation of the Kabala, the Egyptian and Essene mystery schools, and much of New Age. Each representative of the office on this planet has tried to reinforce and expand our understanding of the original teachings.

All those we call the Ascended Masters understand the role of the Christ, the qualities of christ consciousness, and the oneness of all things. The Eastern religions openly refer to christ consciousness because they do not see religious lines. One of my memorable moments was reading the opening chapter of *The Life and Teachings of the Masters of the Far East* by Baird Spalding when an Eastern master spoke of the travels of Jesus and John the Baptist to the Far East. This Eastern saint spoke of how the Eastern masters and Jesus shared their teachings and honored the insights they gained from each other.[5]

---

[5] Spalding, Baird, *The Life and Teachings of the Masters of the Far East*, Devross & Co., Camarillo, CA, 1986.

Whether we understand the Christ through the Western or the Eastern approach, understanding the true nature of the Christ helps us break down old dogma and be open to the teachings that lead to Ascension. It took over fifty years of my life for me to fully understand and accept that all the great masters have been teaching the same thing. It was well worth the wait.

Growing Up

I was raised in the Christian church, as most people in the western world have been. I could not have explained what that meant, but I knew what I was supposed to do. I was supposed to go to Sunday school and church and be a good girl. That was fine and dandy until I recognized I could not connect to what I was being taught, had no way to express myself, and began questioning what I was learning.

I have known many people who came into this life fully in touch with their psychic abilities and connection to what lies beyond the physical world. I did not. I did not see auras, talk to angels, or have premonitions of the future as a child. Those skills would come later. I did know myself to be a spiritual being in a way that I did not recognize as unusual or know how to explain as a child. I just knew what I knew, like most children.

After learning that *The Bible* was rewritten and the church reorganized under the non-Christian Roman Emperor Constantine from 314 to 345 A.D., I understood the discrepancies between what I was learning in church and what I felt in my heart. Reading authors such as Elaine Pagels, Lawrence Gardner, and Neil Douglas-Klotz helped me know that my inner voice was right. I had found the road for which I had been searching, and a new world of spiritual evolution opened for me. My heart had indeed opened.

Questioning

Whether we realize it or not, we all know the wisdom of the Christ because christ consciousness is woven into the cellular memory of all humanity. We simply have to wake up and remember who we are to allow that wisdom to come into our conscious minds. What many of us find to be the confines of our various religious teachings do not allow for the universality of the beautiful truths of Jesus, Buddha, Krishna, or the other great spiritual masters who have taught on behalf of the Christ. These teachings have always been here. However, most of us have not been fully exposed to them, and we do not know what we do not know. Therefore, most of us move through our lives with blinders, following the religion to which we were born, until something wakes us up and we begin to ask questions.

For me, the questions began when I was still very young. Some things just did not make sense to me. How could Jesus be the one and only Son of God if we were all supposed to be children of God? How could there be hell when Jesus taught love and forgiveness? Why would God, a loving father, create a bunch of non-Christians so that they would only go to hell (if there was one)? How could there be unconditional love and punishment at the same time? The list of questions went on. It made no sense.

The biggest question for my young mind was that of one and only one life to get it right. If "ashes to ashes and dust to dust" was correct, and there were cycles of life, what about the human soul? If everything else got recycled, why didn't we? I was sure something was missing.

I remember the first day I heard someone speaking about reincarnation. I was only ten years old, but I knew I had just listened to the truth. I did not know what to do with that truth, but I packed it away for the future, assuming I would figure it all out someday. Many years later, I learned that reincarnation had been part of the original teachings of Jesus but was removed from *The Bible* as part of the "reorganization" of the church. In defiance of Emperor Constantine, many priests actively taught reincarnation as part of Christian doctrine until 553 A.D., when Rome declared ex-communication for anyone continuing that practice. While this knowledge raised even more questions about the Bible's accuracy, I had at least one question answered.

I continued to participate in church as a youngster, but I could not find the answers to my questions or the connection to the Christ that I sensed but could not define. Going to college was the perfect opportunity to separate from church almost entirely. I did not lose my desire to know the Christ better, but with no specific direction to follow, I put my spiritual interests on the back burner and went on about my life as most young adults seem to do. I read a few good spiritually based books over the years and learned to meditate, but gradual exploration was all I wanted for many years.

Learning to Meditate

Part of my gradual spiritual exploration in my thirties was learning Transcendental Meditation. My first experience was the bliss of feeling my connection to what I called the universe. The purpose of meditation is to transcend the lower-self (the physical, emotional, and mental self) to experience the spiritual-self. Until one quiets the mind, the emotions, and the body, one cannot know a full connection to one's soul. As *The Bible* says, "Be still and know that I am God!"[6]

Once I got used to being in the stillness, I began to get messages from my soul. The stillness is where we hear our true inner voice, or divine guidance, as long as we are clear and willing to listen. For me, that guidance began as messages when I was coming out of the meditative state. My mind was relaxed and open at that time, so my soul could slip me a message without my lower-self interfering and talking me out of it.

I found the messages I received coming out of meditation were right on target. No matter what I was guided to do, it worked perfectly. Over time, I learned to connect and receive clear guidance at any time and to trust that connection.

The importance of meditation cannot be over-emphasized. No one has ascended from this planet without becoming a master of meditation. In the deep meditative state, we experience ourselves beyond the illusion of the physical world. In other words, in the deep meditative state, you experience your true self—your self-as-Source.

The goal is to reach the avatar state of walking meditation—the state of ever-present oneness with Source. However, that does not happen without the mastery of traditional meditation.

---

[6] Psalms 46:10, *NRSV Bible with the Apocrypha*, Kindle Edition, HarperCollins, New York, NY, 2011.

The Big Awakening

I had my big awaking, the one I could not ignore, in August 1999. I had become interested in self-healing through energy work and was exploring various options. My husband and I were living in Colorado. I enrolled in a class on healing techniques in Denver, expecting the focus to be on learning to heal the physical body with some emphasis on the emotional, mental, and spiritual aspects.

I was already enjoying the class when the teacher announced that we would begin healing past lives. We were to use a specific technique to identify a time in the past that needed healing and clear it. My enjoyment changed to anticipation as I expected something very exciting to happen. I had always believed in reincarnation and had read about healing the present life by healing past lives. I was ready for the experience.

Most of the people in the room were getting immediate results. They were identifying lives that needed healing and going to work. I listened to the stories people shared around the room, but I sat dead in the water. Nothing was coming for me. I so wanted a past life experience, and I was getting nothing. My anticipation began to turn to frustration, but I was determined enough not to give up. I tried one more time to locate a past life to clear. I so wanted this to happen.

I cannot say what life I tapped into, but suddenly I was overcome with emotion. I felt so weak I had to put my head down on the table. My back began to boil. The instructor came over and tried to touch my back, but it was too hot. This energy continued for a couple of minutes at most. Then, as though a veil was lifted, all the intensity flowed away. I was exhilarated and full of joy. The only thing I knew was that the people who were my mother and father in this life were somehow involved in that past life and that all the old energy had been cleared away. Wow!

The doors opened, and I instantly knew the next step on my path was to learn more about past lives, how they affected current lives, and how to heal them. It all seemed so completely natural that I could hardly believe I had not gotten this sooner. But, now that I was awake, I was going to keep moving.

Being new to all this, I was not sure of how to proceed. The guidance I had gotten in my modest meditations had always been on target, so I went back to my meditation chair for answers. I was directed in meditation to a course on past lives, energy structure, and clearing discordant energy that I had encountered in the class I had just taken. A teacher in that particular practice had just moved to my area, and I was able to get started right away. There are no accidents.

I was so excited. I threw myself into my studies and could not learn fast enough. I spent hours each day working on myself and my friends to learn as much as I could. I was amazed at the results I was getting from healing myself and others. I could not slow down. I began taking on paying clients for private sessions, and it felt good.

Many forms of service are required to move humanity forward into divine community and living in oneness. The teacher/healer is only one of those, but it has filled my heart with incredible joy. Other people will find their joy by brightening our lives with art, growing our food, or building our homes, but my joy is through helping others discover the divine within and teaching them how to fully experience the truth of who they are as Source.

The Next Step

I had many important teachers during the early stages of my journey. Each was special, and each served me well for what I needed at the time. After my profound experience in August 1999, I was ready for yet another change in direction.

I was guided in a meditation to Kris Duffy and I Am Source™. Through these teachings, I found the next step in my evolution. Working with Kris, I gained a new understanding of the Christ and spiritual mastery for which I had searched. I began teaching the program in May 2000 and never looked back.

There are many roads to the Buddha, and I knew this one to be mine. It is not that I never looked at other programs and techniques because I did. A good teacher must also be a good student, and you never know where you might find a real gem of wisdom or a technique that resonates with your energy. However, I never found anything that spoke to me as clearly and completely as what I learned from Kris.

I Am Source™ taught what the title says, that we are each Source. We are each the God/Goddess in human form with all the attributes and powers of the divine. In this program, the Christ taught that he is not our source. He is a teacher.

This concept is challenging for many with a strong Christian background. A big eye-opener for me was the words of Unity minister Eric Butterworth in his book *Discover the Power Within You: a guide to the unexplored depths within*. Dr. Butterworth wrote that there was a difference between the religion *of* Jesus and the religion *about* Jesus.[7] How true this was for me.

I have mentioned that I gained new insight into the Christ through my studies. The phrases "I am the light and the way" and "the only begotten Son" were created and added to *The Bible* and church doctrine more than 300 years after the life of Jesus.

Bishops and priests protesting the changes wrote many letters to the emperor. They asked, what gave Constantine the right to change church doctrine? Jesus called himself a teacher, not the only begotten Son. He sought to empower others, not to make them servants to the church. However, fighting the Emperor of Rome was no use, and the course of the Christian religion was changed by a non-Christian man who had the power to have done what he wanted to have done.

As I listened to Kris teach, I felt as though I was hearing the real voice of the Christ for the first time. Everything I *thought* I knew began to make sense, and the course of my life changed. I was on my road to becoming a teacher.

---

[7] Butterworth, Eric, *Discover the Power within You, a guide to the unexplored depths within*, Harper and Row, New York, NY, 1968.

My Choice of New Age to New Thought

No matter which road you choose to follow, the same basic principles and understandings must be mastered for Ascension. These principles and understandings have been taught in one form or another since the beginning of time on the planet. However, we have a never-ending need for these teachings to be shared by many voices in many ways. The words that speak clearly to one person may sound like gibberish to another. As our consciousness changes, we need a higher understanding of what we have heard before, so we search for new teachers. And the beat goes on.

The beat I dance to in this life is New Age or New Thought. These categories are not the same, but they overlap and have many similarities. The biggest issue is that we have to label any spiritual paths or philosophies because many of us do not fit into anyone's box.

I have had many lives as Hindu, Buddhist, Christian, and others to test the waters of my evolution. I have loved them all, and they each had a great purpose. Having integrated most of those teachings, I have been led to a less defined path in the final stages of the Experiment in Duality.

There is, of course, nothing new about either New Age or New Thought. They are merely the newest versions of an old song, but the versions that ring true for many of us seeking the understanding that has eluded us on the more traditional paths. I cherish what I have learned from the traditional spiritual teachings of both the East and the West. I incorporate them into my life every day. They truly never grow old. I even have hand mudras and chants that emerge from my cellular memory of my Eastern lives, which I use with great benefit for myself and my students. It is fun to remember all that we are.

It is important to remember that all the great traditions—Egyptian, Essene, Sufi, Sikh, Hindu, Buddhist, Christian, and more—have given rise to ascended masters even though they often differ in specific beliefs, theories, and processes. Buddha veered away from the gods and goddesses of Hinduism and taught that there is only the God-Within. Hinduism still speaks of many gods and goddesses to support and assist followers on their road. These are very different philosophies, yet both ancient traditions have given us ascended masters because they are both based on finding unconditional love and oneness with all things.

Even within Hinduism, there are two divergent teachings on sexuality and Ascension. One set of beliefs says that celibacy (removing oneself from carnal experiences) is the fastest way to Ascension. The other says that mastering the spiritual aspects of sexuality through the study and practice of Tantra (merging the male and female into spiritual, not just physical, bliss) is the fastest way. Amazingly, they both work!

While Buddha said to be a lamp unto oneself and not to search for light anywhere else, he also said that we are all students and teachers for one another at all times. There are many roads to Ascension, and our diversity should make this process more enlightening, not create separation.

For me, the teachings in the original I Am Source™ program and the channelings from my soul have given me an understanding that has catapulted me beyond what I thought possible when I began my conscious road to Ascension. The most important skill you can learn is to be a clear channel for guidance from your soul—the Source within.

The critical word here is *clear.* It is all too easy to get "guidance" from the lower-self and hear what makes the lower-self comfortable instead of what is needed and what is in the highest good. It is through following your guidance that you find your answers and your way home to the light. The ability to know if you are getting clear guidance is essential. The teachings from the Christ gave me techniques I had not encountered in my previous studies.

I admit that I was not accustomed to associating the Christ with New Age. I had a bit of disconnection between my many lives as a "Christian" and what I was learning in New Age teachings. My soul guided me to do research for a book my soul wanted me to call *Jesus: The First New Ager* to help me sort it out in my mind. I knew the plan was not for me to write this book but to do the research that would help me get past some of my old dogma relative to the Christ and open me to more acceptance of what I had been learning about the Experiment in Duality.

The project was fascinating. I read portions of *The Bible*, the Nag Hammadi Library, other "lost gospels," and various channelings from the Archangels and the Ascended Masters. When comparing these writings to what

I had read from the masters of the East, the message was always the same—we are Source. If we are born of the God/Goddess, we *must* have all the qualities, aspects, and powers of the God/Goddess. This power has always been the message of the Office of the Christ. We are all part of the God/Goddess/All That Is. We are Source. Anything else is the illusion.

Getting to Here

We are always on our spiritual path. No matter how much light or "dark" we hold, we are always on that path because, at heart, we are spiritual beings in pursuit of our true selves.

The guy at the back of the conga line, whom I affectionately refer to as "the densest post," is on their spiritual path but just does not know it. At some point, we each wake up and consciously choose to pursue the spiritual self. Kris always said that we each had a time-release capsule inside, and when it was time, it opened. I had my experience in August 1999. I woke up and jumped full speed ahead into my spiritual evolution. I cannot tell you how I did it. I just knew it was time. I guess my capsule was ready to open.

I do not know how I could have gotten to where I am without New Age philosophy. Separating what I learned as a child from what I felt in my heart to be true was not easy. The Eastern teachings appealed to me but seemed either too intense or too esoteric for me to follow in the beginning, although I understand and truly appreciate them now. The ideas of the New Age seemed to ring true to me and the best place for me to begin.

However, I do not agree with all New Age philosophies and principles. People who wear the same label can have widely varying beliefs and opinions. All Democrats do not think and believe alike. All Republicans do not think and believe alike. All Christians, all Jews, all Hindus, etc., do not think and believe alike. Whether political, religious, or otherwise, the people of a particular group may share a similar foundation, but their specific beliefs and opinions vary.

The New Age community is no different. The name New Age encompasses a wide range of philosophies and beliefs. There are many voices to be heard and many approaches to explore. While I found much in my first venture into New Age that was right for me, I also found much that was not. I kept studying until I found the pieces that fit me and the direction I was guided to take. My guidance has always led me to the right place.

When I teach, I offer what I have learned and what has served me on my road to where I am now. I ask my students to hold an open heart and an open mind for the possibility that what I have to share may be true and may be of service to them. If it rings true, they are to keep it and use it. If it does not, they are to toss it away. First and foremost, they must learn to trust their own guidance.

Trusting your guidance is a skill and is often intimidating to many who usually wait for wisdom from the teacher. But, as we say in the New Age, the day of the guru is over. The day of waiting for the teacher to tell us what to do is over. The day of giving away our power to the teacher has passed. How do you learn to trust your inner voice if you do not practice trusting?

We must all learn to go within for our answers and our truth. My dear friend and long-time student, Sarah, once told me (with laughter in her voice), "I am often envious. My friends tell me their teachers gave them advice and told them what to do. When I ask you what I should do, you tell me go to my guidance. You make *me* figure it out!"

Letting Go of Judgment and Dogma

At one time, I thought I would write a book just about the Christ and the role that Jesus played as a representative of the office. However, *The Yoga of Jesus* by Yogananda says much of what I would have said. It is an excellent example of crossing spiritual disciplines to find the unity of the sacred teachings.[8] While some of the Hindu perspectives that Yogananda put forth in his book are not my truth, this book is an excellent read for those trying to sort out the original teachings of Jesus versus the traditional interpretations that most of us in the West have learned. I believe Yogananda found the authentic voice of the Christ.

---

[8] Paramahansa Yogananda, *The Yoga of Jesus,* The International Publications of Self-Realization Fellowship, Los Angeles, CA, 2007.

Non-judgment is absolutely key. Kris once taught a class titled "Judgment: THE Block to Experiencing Oneself as God." Judgment in *any* form is separation. Yet almost every religion has taken on its set of judgments. Christianity and Judaism have their heaven and hell. Buddhism and Hinduism have what are perceived as the rewards and punishments of the karmic debt system. Other religions have theirs as well.

Moving past these old judgments, and breaking down the walls between us, as Yogananda did, is not as easy as it might seem on the surface. We have to let go of so much dogma. No matter what we say we believe in our conscious minds, the teachings of the past are very entrenched in our subconscious. Until the old beliefs are healed at the subconscious level, the subconscious mind controls more of our lives than our conscious mind does. Healing the layers of dogma can take time and patience, but it can and must be done to allow space for the energy that will lead to the end of separation and the Experiment in Duality. So, embrace the process. I did.

The Experiment in Duality

Once I understood my spiritual path from a new perspective, it was much easier for me to put the pieces of my puzzle together. Understanding the Experiment in Duality, what we are doing here, and why, opened up a new world of possibilities. Understanding the Experiment in Duality helped me put all the stories in perspective. I could put every creation story into the format of the experiment and understand it. I could begin to look at everyone and everything with greater compassion, understanding, forgiveness, and love. Understanding the experiment and my role in it allowed me to release the judgment of myself and others much more quickly than I believe I could have done on another path of study.

The Archangels and Ascended Masters started teaching about the Experiment in Duality, or the Great Experiment, in the 1920s. However, these teachings were relatively brief and did not provide enough for me to gain the depth of understanding I seemed to need to crawl out of the judgment.

Just as I teach others to do, I went to my soul for the answers. By channeling to my soul and the Christ, I began to understand the experiment in a way that served me. I began to accept that separation was not our truth, but our illusion. I began to accept that all I needed to do was put the entire experience on earth into the perspective of Source and learn to let it go.

Source sees everything through the eyes of divine love and forgiveness. While humans hold judgment on what is right or wrong, Source has no judgments on our choices. Where humans see good or bad, Source sees only opportunities for growth and expansion. Source holds the space for creative expression and exploration and allows us to find our way. Source sees the light coming out of our journey into darkness. Source sees us as beautiful children. We have to do the same.

It truly is simple, but simple is not the same as easy. We have many lifetimes of false beliefs and limiting perceptions to overcome to accept the simplicity of it all. However, if we keep taking one step at a time, we will each get there. One needs persistence, patience, and non-judgment throughout the spiritual process, so just keep on trucking.

Ascension

Ascension means different things to different people. As I discuss in the next chapter, there is the process of ascension (raising one's frequency) and the final Ascension from the cycles of reincarnation on this planet.

From our first incarnation on this planet to the last, we are continually evolving—moving from beliefs in separation to reunification with Source. Lifetime after lifetime, we experience, evaluate, learn, and go around again until we have learned all that we can learn from life on earth. When we can only continue to expand our love beyond the human experience, we are ready for our final Ascension.

In the past, when we made the final ascension from our human bodies to continue our evolution without bodies, we would still be inside the experiment because the upper dimensions of ourselves, the non-physical dimensions of ourselves, were also inside the experiment. However, the experience of duality was less dense in the upper realms and easier to heal. We could continue healing the separation in the etheric realms until our process was complete.

The experiment is now over in the upper dimensions of who we are. We have only to allow that healing to filter down to who we are here on the planet, wrap up the remaining energies of duality in our physical world, and find ourselves in our light. The experiment has stretched as far as it can, and we have the chance, and the choice, to step out of it completely. The opportunity to end duality forever is finally here.

Kris used to equate this concept to the experience of some Japanese soldiers at the end of World War II. For years after the end of the war, Japanese soldiers were found on isolated Pacific islands with no awareness that the war was over. They had spent years alone, not knowing they could go home. It is time for each of us to know "the war" is over, and we can go home, and we can go home now.

We are all at different points in our process of ending duality. Whether one is just awakening to their conscious spiritual growth or whether one has been actively pursuing spiritual evolution for a long time, we always have more to learn. Something has guided you to this point in your life. Listen to that inner voice, and it will guide you to your next step.

Embrace your ascension no matter what path you choose to follow. Do not let anyone or anything hold you back from the truth of who you are. Do not let anyone or anything to tell you that you are not Source. Do not let anyone or anything stop you from knowing the bliss of oneness and Ascension to the next realm.

Chapter 3

Ascension and the Experiment

as·cen·sion n., the act of rising or ascending; especially, the act of moving to a higher point or more powerful position
—*Random House Webster's College Dictionary*

Much has been written and spoken about Ascension, which means there are various versions of what Ascension means. I find it easiest to understand when I break it down into *ascension* with a small *a* and *Ascension* with a capital *A*.

Ascension is both a process and a destination. Ascension with a small *a* is the process of moving back into the remembrance of ourselves as pure light and pure love by raising our frequency. It is the continuous movement through various stages of spiritual evolution over many lifetimes. It is not just "moving to a higher or more powerful position" as the dictionary defines it. It is moving to a higher frequency, which means a higher level of understanding of oneself as Source.

However, the time will come for each of us when we can no longer continue our evolution in a physical body because the physical form cannot hold enough light. At some point, the only way to continue evolving is to graduate to the next stage of our evolution, beyond the physical form—Ascension with a capital *A*.

If we look at ascension as the act of moving higher in frequency through our human evolution, then we have always been ascending. We have always been on our spiritual path. We have been moving back toward the light since the beginning.

When we each decided to join the experiment on earth, we packed a spiritual suitcase for what we wanted to learn and jumped in line to join the party. Everyone did not come in at once. Some have been here since the beginning of human life on this planet, and others joined the party later. Hence, the conga line.

Each time we reincarnated, we packed a new suitcase of gifts and talents, lessons to learn, and items to clear for each new life. Each life was meant to expand our experience and allow us an opportunity to perfect something we might have missed the last time around.

When looking at someone's behavior, you do not know what that person has packed in their suitcase for this life or why, and you do not know where that person is in the conga line—great master or dense post. You only know what you see and hear until you use your connection to the source within to discern.

The Goal

We have always been in the process of ascension, moving into higher and higher frequencies of love and oneness, even though it has not always felt that way. As we move into the higher frequencies of love, our memories become clearer, and we begin to long for the experience of oneness with All That Is. Our goal is to graduate from the experiment by ending duality and experiencing the state of being we knew before we came into the experiment.

The Tibetans have a saying that you cannot get off the wheel of reincarnation until you love it on Earth so much you no longer feel the need to leave. We cannot stay here forever because we are meant to graduate and move on. We are designed to seek higher and higher frequency experiences. However, we must stay until we heal all judgments about what we have created inside the experiment. If one's goal is to escape, one does not yet understand. When we no longer hold judgment on our experiences here, and we love being here as much as we could love being anywhere else, we have healed the duality and can move on at any time. While the ascended masters who have gone before us found their way back to oneness, any path in New Age will be easier with a better understanding of the experiment, why we entered into it, and what we can do to end it.

Time to Surrender

Duality is a temporary condition. We are in an experiment about the perception of separation from Source. While this experiment began with the highest intentions, it created great turmoil and caused us to forget that we are one. The key to quickly ending the experience of duality is seeing it for what it is without judgment or blame.

The challenge is that we have resided inside the experiment for so long that we have come to believe that the world we have been experiencing is the reality instead of remembering that this is only the format we created to learn about separation, *not* the real deal. Nothing in this 3rd-dimensional realm is real, but we believe it is. Overcoming this perception has proven to be a bigger task than expected, but it no longer needs to be. We simply need to understand what is going on so that we can surrender. It is white flag time. Understanding is the easy piece; surrendering is more challenging.

Many believe that the Experiment in Duality has only occurred here on earth. It has, however, been experienced on the planets and stars of multiple galaxies. Some of these planets and stars have already completed the experiment and returned to oneness, as we will soon do on earth. Some of our friends from other planets and stars are still caught in the illusion like we are. They still fight for control over others, including us. However, those who have returned to their light are here to be our teachers and are working with the Office of the Christ to bring us home.

The Illusion of Duality

Many people believe that duality is the battle between good and evil, the fight between light and dark. Others believe duality is the separation of the male and female. It is neither. The perception of light and dark is an illusion. The separation of male and female energies is also an illusion. These are the results of our experiences inside the experiment. They are symptoms of duality, not duality itself.

The real illusion of duality is the belief that we are separate from Source. Duality is defined in the experiment as the duality of wills—the separation of Divine Will from the little will of man. Before the experiment, we had only one will, one desire—for the highest good of all. In the flow of oneness, the highest good of the whole ultimately creates the highest good of the individual parts.

For example, any sports fan knows when watching a game if a team is in the flow or it is not. When a team is in the flow, working together unselfishly for the team's highest good, it is a beautiful thing to watch. When a team is not in the flow, acting as individuals and competing with each other to be seen as the star, it is not a beautiful thing to watch. It is a mess. The first creates unity; the other creates division.

To create separation for the experiment, we invented the concept that the individual parts did not need to consider each other. We shifted the focus from the highest good of the whole to the desires of the individual. We lost teamwork and created individual players—winners and losers.

Merging your little will with Divine Will for the highest good of all is how you end duality. Surrendering to Divine Will is how you experience oneness with Source and expand who you are. Surrendering creates incredible joy and freedom that cannot be experienced when bound to the little will of man.

The Physical Illusion

The physical world, as we know it, is not real. The physical world may look and feel real, but it is not. Whether one listens to the masters of the ancient mystery schools or the scientists of today's quantum mechanics, one will be presented with the facts to show that the physical world is not really here. What appears to be solid is simply a collection of spinning atoms. These atoms are made of subatomic particles spinning so fast that they appear to be solid, just as the blades of a quickly spinning fan appear to be a solid circle. Subatomic particles break down into even smaller pieces of energy until nothing solid exists.

Everything from the air we breathe to the food we eat to the bodies we inhabit is pure energy brought into form for the experience of learning more about creation and the unlimited possibilities of Source. Yes, the physical world is an illusion, but that is not the illusion we need to resolve. When we resolve the illusion that we are separate from Source, the illusion of the physical world will resolve itself.

The fear of accepting the physical world as an illusion is that we do not remember ourselves as pure energy. The universe outside the experiment also exists in the "illusion" of a physical world. However, the beings living outside the experiment experience their physical "reality" in alignment with the God/Goddess/All That Is and Divine Will. They experience their world as the metaphorical Garden of Eden.

Only inside the experiment do we experience the duality of wills and the perception of separation from Source. Only inside this illusion do we experience the perception of the light and dark or the separation of the male and female. Only inside the experiment do we perceive the physical world as all there is and, therefore, rely on the physical world for our safety and security. This perception must change for us to move back into oneness and ascend.

The Perception of Separation

Duality is not the battle between light and dark or the separation of the male and female. The perception of light and dark and the perception of separation of the male and female are simply two expressions of duality. Once we decided to participate in this experiment, we had the choice in each life to follow the little will of man or to follow Divine Will. As we made choices to follow the little will instead of Divine Will, we created a separation between the lower-self and Source. The more choices we made to follow the little will, the greater our perception of separation.

The choice to move away from the light created a split within human consciousness. We began to *feel* ourselves as separate. This feeling of separation from Source created the perception of light and dark within ourselves and, therefore, the perception of light and dark in the world around us. The feeling of separation also created the perception of separation between the male and female, a severance of our male and female archetypes. That separation projected itself into the outer world as the battle between the sexes. When the duality within *ourselves* is healed, everything else will fall into place.

The Purpose

Why did we do it? What was the purpose of creating an experiment in duality? How, as many feel, did we go so far into darkness? Understanding what we are doing here and why we did it will help you move back into your mastery of oneness.

The purpose of the experiment was to expand our capacity for unconditional love. The idea may seem a stretch at first, and many may find it ridiculous. However, remember to hold open the possibility that what I have to share may be true before discarding it.

As beings of great light, we know that love is our entire existence and purpose. As our love grows, we grow. Therefore, we are always seeking new ways to create and experience higher frequencies of divine love, love with no judgments and no conditions.

Between lifetimes, we evaluate what we have learned and what our next steps could be. One of us began asking if there was something new we could do to expand our experience of love. All we had ever known was the Divine. When everyone treats everyone else with respect, unconditional love is easy. When no one does harm, non-judgment is easy. But what if everyone did not come from oneness or the highest good of all? If we were able to create the experience of non-love, what might we learn from it? Would we be able to maintain unconditional love even in non-loving circumstances? Could we move away from divine love and find our way back?

The prospect of an entirely new experience was exhilarating. We had no idea how the separation would feel. We had never known ourselves as separate from Source or separate from each other. We did not know where this idea would take us. Still, we were excited about the prospect of gaining a greater understanding of ourselves and a greater understanding of unconditional love through experiencing separation. We designed the Experiment in Duality to stretch ourselves, challenge ourselves, and expand our capacity for unconditional love. We created it to help ourselves grow.

The process was not easy because it was contrary to our nature. I will share some of the energies we used to create the duality, but, for now, focus on what the experiment means and how it has helped us evolve. Understand that because we created duality, we can change it. You change your beliefs and experiences.

Earth was *an experiment.* No one knew what would happen. We just decided to expand ourselves and try. Now we can bring it to an end. We only have to choose to do it.

One of my fellow facilitators, Nadia, was in a private session with me. We were working on letting go of remnants of the experiment. While she, just like me, had been working on issues surrounding the experiment for a while, she asked, "I know these are judgmental questions but was the experiment worth it? Was it necessary?"

I asked her to get the answer to those questions from her soul for her truth. Her soul replied, "It is not a question of necessary. It was a choice to do something to expand who you were. It was an adventure to help you learn more about yourself."

Then I asked her to ask the God/Goddess how they felt about the experiment. They answered her, "What a journey! If you do not go, you do not know. Look at what you have learned. You are amazing!"

We are all amazing!

We Are All Here by Choice

Everyone here volunteered to be here. Some of us came at the beginning, others were created here, and others joined the experiment in progress, but we all came voluntarily. We came to learn about duality for ourselves and to help others. We could not do this without each other's help. We reflect, or mirror, to each other both the light and the dark inside the experiment to learn about who we are. Working together, we find our way through the maze of separation and back home. It is through our experiences together that we come back into oneness.

Being a volunteer is not always easy. Sometimes we push others' buttons, and sometimes they push ours, but this is how we understand separation versus oneness. It is how we know what we need to heal. It is easy to be in what we think is unconditional love when everything is running smoothly and flowing our way. However, in the test of button-pushing, we discover what we have learned and what we still have to heal.

While it may pain some people to hear this, no one was sent here against their will. The master teachers of this planet have told us since the beginning of time that we have the power of Source and are the creators of our experiences. One cannot be the creator of one's experiences and be a victim at the same time. We cannot be the creators of what we like but not the creators of what we do not like. It is not possible. To accept oneself as part of Source is to accept the power of creatorship and ownership for the choices.

We *are* part of Source. Everything in creation exists *inside* the body of Source. The concept that the creator is "out there" and we are "down here" is part of the illusion of separation. Every new experience expands the knowledge and the wisdom of Source. We are designed and expected to go forth and create.

Psalm 82 of *The Bible* tells us that we were made to be gods. As those whom Source created to be gods, we have the power of creation and choice. Acceptance of that power is liberating. If you accept that you chose to be here, you can choose to heal. You cannot shortcut the process by skipping the steps of ascension, but you have the power and the choice to move through the process as quickly as you choose to do so.

Wanting out due to the judgment about being here is not the answer. Wanting to bring the experience of oneness back to earth is. Feeling we have to appease Source to be welcomed home is not the answer. Knowing that this is our creation and is perfect for this stage of our evolution is. Choosing unconditional love and non-judgment is the way home.

The Desire to Learn

The experiment was not created out of any desire to be separate. The experiment was not intended to bring pain and suffering. It was designed for us to learn from the experience of separation and return to oneness with a greater understanding of unconditional love. Because the perception of separation was the goal, we began to make choices that moved us apart. For the first time, we created the concept of you versus me. We started to make choices based on what the lower-self wanted individually without regard to the effect on the whole.

In the beginning, this was not a challenge. Even though we entered duality in a human body, between lifetimes, we remembered who we were. Between lives, we were able to clear the discordant energies before reentering the experiment. We were able to evaluate what we had learned and decide what to work on next.

However, no one knew what to expect in the long run because nothing like this had ever been done. As we continued the cycles of reincarnation to learn as much as we could, the memories of our light began to dim. We had spent too much time away from home. Eventually, we could no longer clear our energies between lifetimes and started taking the old, dense energies into our new lives. The lower-self could no longer see or feel its light. It could only feel separation, and we began to believe we were lost and alone.

But we are not lost or alone. We only have temporary amnesia.

The Myth of the Darkside

There is no such thing as darkness or "the Darkside." I remember the first time I heard Kris ask, "Have you ever left a room and turned on the dark switch?" Of course, not. There is no dark switch. The lights are either on or off. Darkness is an illusion. What we know as darkness is merely the perception of no light.

No one was created "dark." It is not possible in a universe made of light. Those who have seen the movie trilogy *The Matrix* know that the character Neo loses his physical eyesight at one point and must rely on his inner vision. He is amazed to see that the Machine City, the center of darkness, is actually made of light and only appears dark.[9] Neo's story is our story. There is only light and the perception of no light.

Many entering the experiment chose only to dabble in the separation and go home. That was doable in the beginning because we could clear our energies between our lives and make a choice to return for more education and experience in separation or not. Others entering the experiment chose to learn as much as possible about duality by pushing the envelope and going deeper into duality, thereby creating what we call darkness.

No matter which choice was made, it is important to understand and accept that we *all* "danced with the dark." No one came through the experiment without experiencing separation and "darkness" because that was the point. Whether one danced with the dark a little or a lot does not matter. The dance was just part of the experience. It was just a choice to learn by either scratching the surface or going deep into the experiment.

Let's say that you decide you would like to learn tennis. You buy a racket and an outfit and sign up for lessons. Perhaps all you will ever want to do is play one weekend a month with your friends who also merely wish to dabble in tennis. Or, maybe you will get tennis fever and push yourself to be as good as you can be at the game. These are both fine choices depending on what you want to gain and what you want to experience.

Or, perhaps, you enter an amusement park. As you watch what is happening, you see people who choose to ride the merry-go-round or venture onto the Ferris wheel for a better view and are perfectly happy. Other people, however, decide to push the envelope of thrills and are not satisfied unless they have ridden the scariest ride in the park. Both are excellent choices. They just offer different experiences. The same is true inside the experiment.

Remember that we created separation one choice at a time. Each time we made a choice based on separation instead of oneness, we moved farther from the remembrance of ourselves as light. Those who pushed the envelope by making more and more choices to move away from the light to

---

[9] *The Matrix*, dir. by The Wachowski Brothers (1999; Warner Bros.).

expand their learning eventually crossed an invisible line that left them unable to remember who they were. One moment they could still see home, and the next, they felt hopelessly lost.

This unexpected tumble into darkness left these brothers and sisters completely isolated from the rest of humanity, with no place to go. They found each other wandering in the lack of light, banded together, and began their way of living in a world without the remembrance of love. It was the birth of what is called the Darkside. The Darkside is not real. It never was. It is an aspect of the experiment inadvertently created by the enthusiasm to expand. It merely needs to be healed with love.

There is no *us* versus *them*. The moment you enter into *us* versus *them*, you have stepped backward into separation instead of forward into oneness. We joined this experiment together. Some of us went further than others. That is all. Bless that beloved densest post, the one who has volunteered to anchor the end of the conga line and be the last one through the door home. Somebody has to do it.

Look again at the definition of an experiment: a test, a trial, or a tentative procedure, especially one for the purpose of discovering something unknown or testing a principle or procedure.[10] An experiment is an unknown; otherwise, why do an experiment? We have merely been making one choice at a time based on where we are in our evolution at a given moment. Everyone has been experimenting.

Coming Home

Whether one stepped over the line into the deeper separation or not, the effects of the experiment were the same. Humanity felt alone, afraid, confused, and limited in this strange place that we had created but did not fully understand. We felt abandoned by Source and unable to own that we chose to leave the remembrance of our light. We came to believe we must have done something awful to be left alone like this. Because we could not

---

[10] *Random House Webster's College Dictionary*, Random House, Inc., New York, NY, 1991.

remember our oneness, we began to believe that we were thrown out of heaven by an angry creator.

These feelings of abandonment, and never before experienced density, created inside the experiment gave rise to the story and judgments of Adam and Eve in The Garden of Eden and the Karmic system of rewards and punishments. We have never been bad, never needed to be punished, and never been without Source. We just wandered away from home for a while on a grand adventure and now simply need to decide to go back. Remember, we just have temporary amnesia. It is truly that simple.

The story of The Prodigal Son (the wayward son who returns to his father's loving arms) transcends all religions.[11] No matter what we believe we have done wrong, it is all illusion, and Source eagerly awaits our awakening and our return to oneness. Oneness is the truth of who we are and always will be. Source does not judge our experiences inside the experiment. Only those still stuck in duality hold judgment on what we have done. Understand it, accept it, and let it go.

Because human evolution has never moved as quickly as it is today, many of us are waking up and helping our brothers and sisters remember, too. Hold on to your hats and enjoy the ride home as we continue moving closer to re-establishing oneness on earth.

Mother Earth and the Experiment

Mother Earth and all her kingdoms are part of the experiment. She, like us, chose to participate in this unique adventure for her reasons. She chose to allow her body to be used by us for our evolution. She has loved and supported us through it all and is evolving through her experiences as well.

Humanity could not have done this without her. We have been an integral part of her evolution. Just as the human race is learning to love each other no matter what and move back into oneness, Mother Earth is doing the same. When she has mastered what she is here to learn, the unconditional love of all her children, she will be ready to ascend, too.

---

[11] Luke 15:11-32, *NRSV Bible with the Apocrypha*, Kindle Edition, HarperCollins, New York, NY, 2011.

Remember that duality is not being experienced on earth alone. Just as conflicts, confrontations, and power struggles occurred on this planet, the same energies have played out on other planets and stars throughout the galaxy. Just as human beings became lost, many of our brothers and sisters from the stars did as well. They, too, are learning their way back into oneness.

Accelerating Time

We can end the experiment only through understanding and mastering the mysteries of separation and through reunification with Divine Will. Whether on this planet or another, we must learn what the ascended ones have learned—there is only love. For many years, the Christ, other masters, Archangels, and our friends from the stars who have healed themselves have been teaching and planting seeds to get us ready to complete the experiment. That time is now, and we are ready.

The pace of our evolution is accelerating. Ever since the doors of the mystery schools began to open in the 1930s and 40s, information has flooded the western world. The purpose is to teach westerners what has been taught in the eastern philosophies for centuries. The pace of evolution is increasing to the point where many see that change is now unstoppable. We are heading home, and we are moving quickly.

Many people ask if the experiment is over and we have learned all that we can about separation, why doesn't Source or the God/Goddess or the Christ, or someone else, end it for us? Why don't the Archangels and the Ascended Masters intervene on our behalf and fix this? Why don't they just come down and say, "Game's over, let's go home"? Why do we have to keep doing this on our own?

The answer is that *we are* the experiment. We are the creators, and we still have much to learn by completing what we started. For any experiment, there is planning it, running it, concluding it, and evaluating it. Often, as much is learned during dismantling and reviewing as during the process itself.

The goal is not to get out. The goal is to evolve. The experiment's purpose was to shift into separation and back into oneness with a greater awareness of unconditional love than we knew before we began. Until you have mastered the return, you have not fully understood what you came to learn and have not completed the process.

Source will not take away your power and your opportunity to learn. Growing up is not always easy. The God/Goddess will not take away your mastery by jerking you out prematurely and leaving your process incomplete. Human parents understand that their children need to stretch themselves and learn to stand on their own. Source will allow you to finish what you began, support you in the process, and continue to watch you with non-judgment, love, and detachment.

The Willingness to Change

The process of ending duality and ascending requires changes in how you view yourself and your world and what you do in every moment of your life. I often began classes by saying, "Be ready to accept that everything you have believed to be true is false. The 3rd-dimensional paradigm in which you have lived and the 5th-dimensional paradigm to which you aspire are opposites. As you step onto your spiritual path, you must get ready to turn your world upside down."

Change is not easy for human beings. It is a big deal to ask anyone to change their beliefs and how they have been living their lives. Human beings are very attached to the way things have been. The prospect of change can be daunting, especially in spiritual transformation.

The outer world changes that come with graduating from school, getting married, changing jobs, losing jobs, having children, etc., are challenging enough for most people. Examining one's spiritual beliefs and changing the way one sees oneself in relationship to Source and the rest of humanity is enormous. However, if you view the experiment's creation and conclusion as only climbing down and climbing back up a spiral staircase, change is as easy as taking one small step up at a time.

Chapter 4

The Spiral Staircase

The important thread running through all of these hyperspace considerations is that the laws of nature appear simpler from a higher dimensional perspective
—William A. Tiller, *Science and Human Transformation*

One reason we have so many spiritual philosophies and approaches to Ascension is that there is no one way to describe who we are energetically or how we are moving through the process of raising our frequency. More accurately, it is impossible to do so. Third-dimensional language and structures are limited to what we see, hear, and feel in 3rd-dimensional reality.

To paraphrase Archangel Ariel in *What is Lightbody*, channeled through Tashira Tachi-ren: What we tell you is not the truth. We cannot tell you the truth because you do not have the language or the structure to understand the multidimensional being. We can only give you a guide to finding your way.[12]

Third-dimensional language and structure are dense. Even when using ancient Sanskrit, it is not possible to describe the experiences of the upper dimensions using the 3rd-dimensional languages. When your frequency is

---

[12] Tachi-ren, Tashira and Archangel Ariel, *What is Lightbody,* World Tree Press, Payson, AZ, 1999.

high enough, you begin to *feel* the reality of the upper dimensions. You move beyond the words and charts to experience the simplicity of your multidimensional being. Until then, you must find your way up the road to Ascension using models and metaphors.

The Metaphor of the Spiral Staircase

For me, the best metaphor for our process is seeing the creation of the experiment and its end as climbing down and back up a spiral staircase. Each step represents one rung of frequencies, and each circuit around the spiral equals one octave of frequencies completed.

Everything in creation is pure energy. Each form of energy holds a specific frequency. Because the following terms are often used interchangeably, I will define them for my purpose. These definitions are out of the dictionary but are accurate for metaphysical use.

- *Vibration* is movement. All energy moves. The subatomic particles of each atom in the physical world are always spinning. Each thought and emotion we experience is the result of energy moving through our mental and emotional bodies. Therefore, everything in creation vibrates because everything in creation is moving, whether we have recognized it or not. Movement may be slow or fast.
- *Frequency* is the rate at which something moves. A slow rate of movement is what we call low frequency and feels denser or darker. A fast rate of movement is what we call high frequency and feels lighter or brighter.

Frequency is never good or bad. It simply is. A slower, denser frequency holds less light and therefore feels darker and less loving. A faster, higher frequency has more light and therefore feels brighter and more loving. One is not better than the other, but one certainly feels better than the other. It is merely a matter of experience based on where one stands on the scale of frequencies.

Using sound is the simplest way to understand the scale of frequencies. Every musician understands the scale of sound. Whether playing the piano or flute or using the human voice, each sound holds a place on the scale. An octave of sound is eight notes: A-B-C-D-E-F-G-A. On the scale, the last A begins the next octave, and the octaves keep climbing higher.

The piano is a perfect model. Every keyboard has its lowest note A and its highest note A. The octave, or pitch, depends on the length of the piano string. The longest A-string vibrates the slowest and produces the lowest octave of the note A. As a pianist plays up the octaves on the keyboard, the A-strings get shorter, and the frequency, or pitch, of A goes higher.

When listening to music, we hear the low octaves as dark and ominous and the higher octaves as light and fun. The musical masterpiece *Peter and the Wolf* by Sergei Prokofiev is a perfect example.

On the spiral staircase, each step is a note on the frequency scale of evolution. Each circuit around the staircase completes an octave of frequency. Climbing down the stairs creates a denser, less loving experience, while climbing up the stairs creates a brighter, more loving one. Therefore, everything you do that creates or holds low frequency keeps you in the illusion of darkness and separation, and everything you do that creates or holds high frequency moves you back toward your truth as light and love.

Creating Density

Returning to the conga line metaphor, imagine us getting ready to enter the experiment. We had to design and climb down the spiral staircase. We each had to lower our frequency from divine love and oneness to create the concept of separation.

Once we had constructed the staircase, everyone who chose to participate got in line to climb down into the experiment. Step by step, the conga line descended. Every step into a lower frequency allowed us to create a new level of separation. We locked our upper chakras to block our light and scrambled our DNA to forget who we were. We created false beliefs of separation to create limitations, made vows and contracts to block our memories, and more so that we could have the full experience of the Experiment in Duality.

Climbing back up the staircase is as simple as doing whatever you need to do to hold higher and higher frequencies and remember that you are, and have always been, divine. Understanding the process of shifting through the lower dimensions of consciousness makes that process easier.

Shifting Dimensional Perspective

The ascension process requires shifting dimensional consciousness and merging the lower-self with the self-as-Source, or the soul. On this planet, we are moving from the 3rd to the 4th to the 5th dimensional level of consciousness. This shift is a step-by-step process that requires many levels of learning.

The word *dimension* is another word used in many ways. When I first began my serious spiritual studies, I heard the terms 3rd, $4^{th,}$ and 5th-dimensional consciousness used quite often, but no one I asked could fully explain them to me. Again, many thanks to the Christ and Kris Duffy for giving me an explanation that is still used in the Standing in the Light® program today.

Standing in the Light® uses a twelve-dimensional model to explain the levels of consciousness. We must move from the density of our lower-self up to the light of our self-as-Source. I will discuss only the 3rd, $4^{th,}$ and 5th dimensions of consciousness here because those pertain to the discussion of ascension from the human form. This model is used widely in the New Age community. In this model, the 3rd and 4th dimensions of consciousness are mastered in the physical body. Reaching full 5th-dimensional consciousness is Ascension.

When we descended the staircase, we dropped our consciousness from that of oneness to that of separation. We forgot that we were Source and began to believe that we were only human. To move back into the experience of oneness, we have to climb out of 3rd-dimensional consciousness, through 4th-dimensional consciousness, and into 5th-dimensional consciousness. Each of these dimensions has multiple octaves of frequencies and experiences through which to evolve.

At the lowest octave of the 3rd-dimensional level of consciousness, we perceive ourselves as separate beings, disconnected from the rest of humanity. The goal at this level of consciousness is to take care of oneself; in other words, to take care of *me* and *my* needs. At the lower end of 3rd-dimensional consciousness, the outer world, the physical world, is All That Is real, and getting our needs met in that world is all that counts. At this level, the lower-self focuses on its safety, security, survival, and pursuit of a bigger piece of the pie. Not only does the lower-self want to be sure it has enough, but it also wants more than enough if it can get it.

At the 5th-dimensional level of consciousness, we have raised our frequency high enough to remember that we are part of the whole. The concept of separation has been healed, and the goal has shifted from taking care of *me* to taking care of *us*.

The 5th-dimensional self is motivated by the desire to help everyone heal and remember that they are Source. In 5th-dimensional consciousness, we know that the highest good of all is always in the individual's highest good, too. At this frequency, we understand that if we are all one, what helps or hurts one of our brothers or sisters also helps or hurts us. We understand that no one's physical, emotional, or mental needs should go unmet. Most importantly, no one's spiritual evolution should be ignored. This shift is the experience of bringing oneness back to earth and seeking divine harmony, cooperation, unity, and oneness.

It is a long journey from the depths of the 3rd dimension to the heights of the 5th dimension. Fourth-dimensional consciousness is the transition between the two. It is the beginning of the shift of consciousness from *me* to *us*. It is where we learn how to move from the world of the lower-self into the world of the self-as-Source. The 4th dimension is challenging because we don't know what to do there. We understand how to live in the third-dimensional world, and the people there understand us. As we start to break away from the old paradigm and move toward our fifth-dimensional consciousness, our friends and relatives do not understand us anymore, and we can feel very alone.

The 4th-dimensional portion of our road to Ascension is both exhilarating and scary. We do not have a clear road map for this part of the journey, so finding a program and process right for us is important. I say, just fasten your seatbelt and enjoy the ride!

Ascension is Really Descension

When we began our journey down the spiral staircase, our energy structure was that of pure light. The farther down the staircase we traveled, the more our structure changed. These changes have been represented graphically in spiritual teachings since the beginning of time. The following symbols have been used for millennia to represent our journey. The upward-pointing triangle, or pyramid, represents 3rd-dimensional consciousness and the downward-pointing triangle, or pyramid, represents 5th-dimensional consciousness.

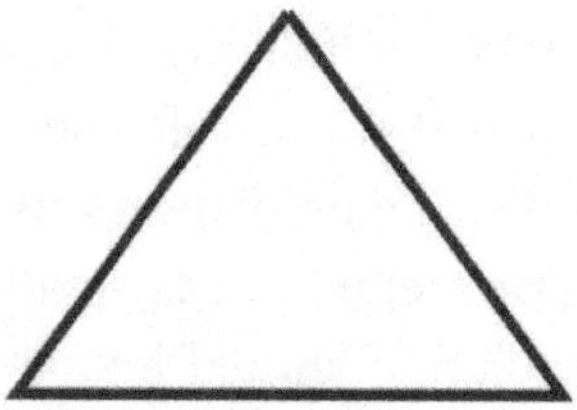

3-D Consciousness

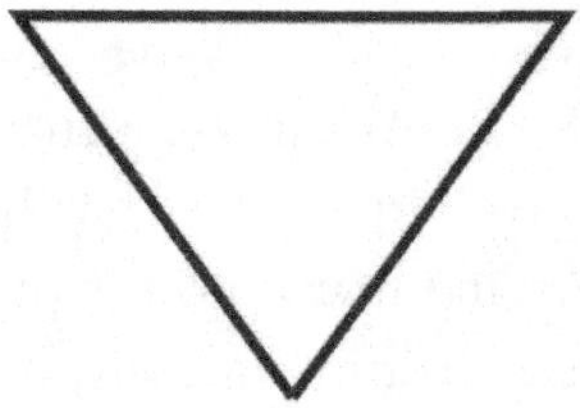

5-D Consciousness

At the beginning of our journey, we experienced our physical form in unity and oneness with all things. Like the metaphor of Adam and Eve in the Garden of Eden before the apple, we knew ourselves as divine. The double tetrahedron represented our energy. In this symbol, the consciousness of the physical body sits atop the soul's consciousness, representing the oneness of the two worlds. "Biting the apple" was the first step down the staircase.

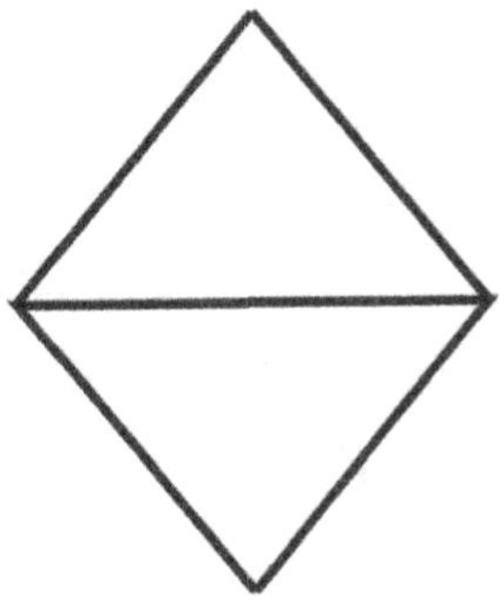

5-D Double Tetrahedron

As we descended the staircase into the experiment, our frequency began to drop, and our energy became denser. The 3rd-dimensional pyramid on top got heavy and began to sink. We were losing the memory of who we were. This loss of frequency created the Star of David, where we had one foot in the upper paradigm and one foot in the lower paradigm.

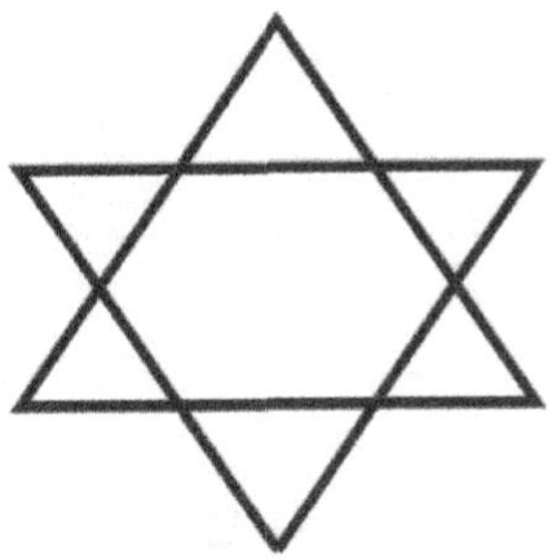

4-D Star of David

When we reached the bottom of the staircase, we had completely forgotten we were one and perceived ourselves as separate from Source. Our heart chakras were closed, and the only belief in any god that might exist was that he must be *up there,* and we were stuck *down here.*

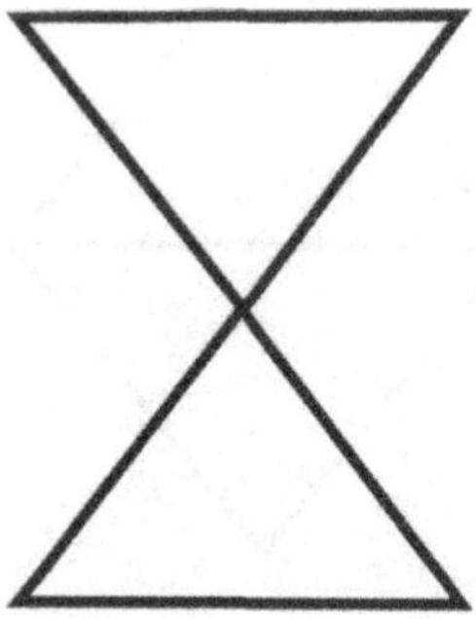

3-D Hourglass

Putting this together, we have a graphic representation of our shift from oneness into separation.

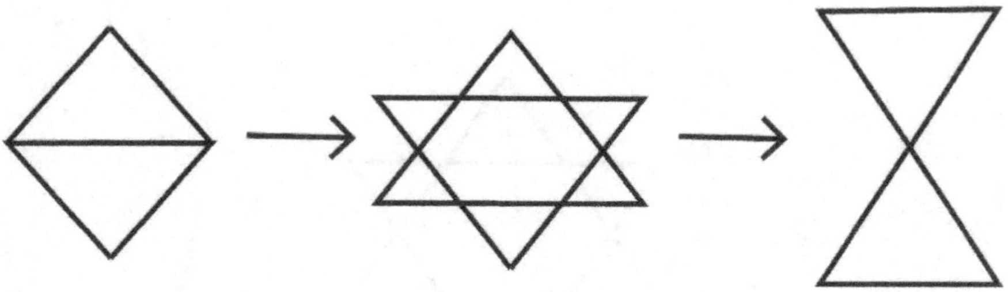

5-D **4-D** **3-D**

When we look at reversing the process, we see that ascension is really descension. We must raise the frequency of the lower-self high enough to allow our souls to descend into our energy field. At first, the frequency of the lower-self rises slowly. As the 3rd-dimensional pyramid gets lighter, the 5th-dimensional pyramid can begin to descend, again creating the Star of David pattern. As the lower-self continues to raise its frequency, the self-as-Source represented by the 5th-dimensional pyramid can completely descend, creating the full experience of oneness and the end of duality.

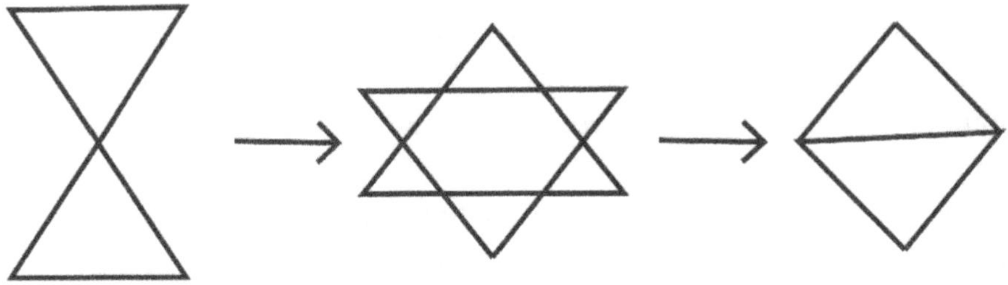

3-D **4-D** **5-D**

Ascension is really the soul's descension into the lower-self's consciousness so that the lower-self remembers and accepts itself as part of All That Is, and the experiment is complete.

Unlocking Our Chakras and Unscrambling Our DNA

To descend the staircase into the experiment, we locked off our upper chakras and scrambled our DNA. Those locks come off as we raise our frequency and reopen our chakras. As we increase our frequency, our DNA remembers and reorganizes itself. So, how does that look?

I have always been guided to the 8-chakra system. In this system, there are seven major chakras in the physical body, with the 8th chakra being the first chakra above the head. The 13-chakra system is also very popular. In this system, there are twelve major chakras in the body, with the 13th chakra being the one above the head. Surprise—they both work. There is also a system that uses only five chakras. It works, too.

It is important to follow your guidance for the system that is right for you and to be sure you are comparing apples to apples and oranges to oranges when you are communicating with others. The 13th chakra means something entirely different to someone working with the 8-chakra system than it does to someone using the 13-chakra system.

A chakra is an energy center. It is a vortex that brings light into the body. When it spins clockwise, it brings energy in; when it spins counter-clockwise, it pushes energy out. Because we are energy beings, the light coming into the body through the chakras is critical. If you think of the chakras as receivers of light, the more chakras you have open and the more open each chakra is, the more light you receive. Light is also known as wisdom. More light coming in means more understanding of spiritual truth and greater insight into using that truth.

In looking at ways to reduce our light for the experience of separation, we blocked the energy coming down the light channel in the center of our bodies by putting locks between specific chakras. In the body, we put locks between the 3rd and 4th chakras, the 6th and 7th chakras, and the 7th and 8th. These are referred to as *the three knots* in Eastern traditions. As one's frequency increases, the locks come off (or the knots untie), and one can access the energy of the next highest chakra. Breaking the lock, or knot, between the 7th and 8th chakras is called breaking through to the thousand petal lotus in Eastern traditions.

We also put locks between each of the chakras above the head—from the 8th up. Once the lock between the 7th and 8th chakras opens, the next phase is to open chakras eight through twelve. The process continues up the light channel to Source. However, that is well beyond anything most people need to focus on now. Considering that most of humanity does not yet have the heart chakra fully open, first things first.

Each chakra has a physical, emotional, mental, and spiritual component. Locking the lower three chakras from the rest of the chakra energy kept human beings in the lower bodies—physical, emotional, and mental. Until the lock between the 3rd and 4th chakras is removed, you cannot access the spiritual energy of the heart. If you cannot access the spiritual energy of the heart, you cannot access higher levels of love and 4th-dimensional consciousness.

If someone is stuck in the energy of the lower three chakras, they are stuck in ego-gratification and the self-serving needs of the lower-self. Those at the end of the conga line are not bad, thoughtless, or selfish. Their behavior is such because they do not hold enough light. The locks are still on their lower chakras, and they cannot act differently. People at the end of the conga line simply need time to catch up to those who have already raised their frequency to the heart level.

We also scrambled and turned off parts of our DNA to forget who we were. While we may have learned in school that our DNA does not change, scientists know better. Studies show that strong emotions, whether negative or positive, shift the structure of the DNA. This ability to change is why people have healed even genetic conditions through laughter and positive imagery.

More parts of human DNA are activating. Children are being born with more codons (the sequence of nucleotides that form a unit of genetic code) activated, immunity to all diseases, and access to psychic skills that have rarely been seen in humans before now. Scientists are revising their beliefs about junk DNA. I loved biology in high school, but I could never understand the concept that our DNA contained useless junk. Just because we do not understand something does not make it useless.

New technologies are opening us to the unlimitedness of human potential. The research is out there, but far beyond the purpose of this book. I encourage anyone guided to see what scientists know today versus what most of us learned in school. It is truly fascinating stuff!

As we ascend the spiral staircase, the changes in our bodies created during our descent and by our experiences on Earth reverse themselves. As human frequency goes higher, our DNA shifts step by step from separation back into its original structure of oneness. This new structure is referred to in New Age as the Original Divine Blueprint. We are going home.

Our Bodies Changed

As the frequencies decreased during the experiment, the structure of the human body changed as well. The unified field of light connected to Source became separated bodies of energy representing the four functions of the human form: physical, emotional, mental, and spiritual. The physical, emotional, mental, and spiritual bodies became separate energy fields with layers of dense energy between them. These layers of density kept the lower bodies in separation and, therefore, stuck in the experiment.

To be one with Source, we must be one within ourselves first. All our bodies must heal their separation and move back into one unified field. The membranes that exist between the lower bodies will be removed, or dissolved, so that the physical, emotional, and mental bodies can merge back into one energy body. Then, the one lower body will merge back into oneness with the spiritual bodies. That unified field will then merge back into oneness with All That Is.

All lower bodies must give up their exclusive territory and realize they are all one. The lower-self cannot exist in any level of separation within itself if it is to move back into oneness with All That Is. You cannot know divine peace and end duality until you have achieved oneness with all you have experienced. This entire experience is an illusion, meaning the outer world can only be healed on the inner. It is always an inside job.

Evolution Means Change

We have always been one with Source. When we speak of "the journey" (or the road or the path) in spiritual circles, we speak of the process of ascension—the process of raising our frequency and remembering who we are as divine love, unity, and oneness. As we descended the spiral staircase, every step was a step lower in frequency, a step away from light and oneness and into the darkness of separation. Each step created change in everything we thought we knew.

The moment you decide to reverse that process and begin climbing back up the staircase, each step is a step higher in frequency (a step away from the darkness into more light), and a change of everything you have come to believe is real inside the experiment. The willingness to change your beliefs and your way of living will determine how quickly you climb out of separation and back into oneness.

When we open ourselves to our spiritual evolution and try to operate by principles we do not yet fully understand, and people around us do not understand, we can feel a bit lost and sometimes a little crazy. Spiritual students often wonder if they are doing the right things and if they will ever get through the process to their mastery. Patience and persistence are keys.

We undergo many changes as we move from who we have been to who we are becoming. It is just part of the process. Evolution means change. Growth means letting go of the old to make room for the new. No one says it is easy to let go, but it does not have to be difficult. The choice is ours to hold on to the old or let go and explore the new.

We each have a personal timetable, and we are allowed to choose our path. The choice is also ours to go fast or slow. One way is not better than another, just different. Make no comparisons. Allow your evolution to be what it needs to be for you.

Chapter 5

Our Stages of Evolution

Everyone wants to evolve,
but no one wants to change.
—Kris Duffy

Evolution means change. One may or may not like it, but change is part of growth. Nothing sits still. Everything is in motion—from the tiniest speck of dust to the largest galaxy in the universe to the universe itself. Everything is in a constant state of change. When we remain still, we become stagnant. If we are stagnant, we are not staying in place; we are falling behind. Anything unwilling to change dies. It is replaced by something new, and evolution continues. Evolution can happen in small steps or all at once, but it always comes.

We can understand the process of evolution by looking at our process of growing up as human beings. Who we are and what we believe when we are six is different from who we are and what we believe when we are sixteen, twenty-six, thirty-six, and so on through our aging process. We know that we continue to change as we grow older because we continue to have new experiences. Each new experience gives us knowledge and wisdom that we did not have before these experiences. This process of human evolution as individuals is the same for nations, economies, philosophies, etc.

The same process of evolution that applies to our human growth applies to our spiritual growth. Evolving from human beings to spiritual beings requires the same growth process as we move from infant to child to adult. Human beings go through multiple stages of evolution over many lives to gain the experiences we need to remember who we are as love and light and overcome separation. We are just children of Source growing up and going through our evolutionary process.

The principles of spiritual evolution are simple, but they require looking at the world through new eyes. We cannot apply the rules of 3rd-dimensional consciousness to our spiritual development. There are parallels, but the 5th dimension operates very differently from what we have experienced in the lower frequencies of the 3rd dimension.

At the 3rd-dimensional level of consciousness, we operate from the desire for ego-gratification and self-preservation in a physical world. This "me first" attitude comes from the belief in separation. At the 5th-dimensional level of consciousness, we operate from the desire for spiritual growth, which means unity and oneness with All That Is. We must be ready and willing to change what we believe and how we do things to make this huge leap in evolution.

Some of us are running toward oneness with open hearts and minds. Some of us are being dragged along, kicking and screaming, through the various stages of evolution. At some point, we must choose to let go of who we have been inside the experiment and rush toward who we are as children of Source. We must attain unity with All That Is to end duality and once again experience a state of oneness. There is no other way home.

How do we make the journey? How do we climb the spiral staircase? The answers to those questions are inside us. They are stored in our cellular memories. We did not come here without a way to get out. However, accessing that information is not always easy when we do not remember who we are, and the lower-self is afraid of change.

Our memories become clearer as we ease the lower-self's fears and allow ourselves to awaken by moving through the various stages of spiritual evolution. Remember, we are simply children of Source growing up and going through our process. We need to give ourselves time to grow into our full potential as Source in physical form.

Stages of Evolution: Growing Up

I mentioned earlier the Eastern saying that the further you go, the more you know you have to learn. That has been my experience over and over again. Just as I begin to believe that I understand divine truth, I jump to the next octave of learning to discover that there is so much more to learn. We can learn much about ourselves and others if we understand that we all move from spiritual infancy to spiritual adolescence to spiritual maturity just as we move through the various stages of our human evolution.

In a human lifetime, we move from birth to death, which may take minutes or years. One is not better than another. They are merely different experiences in the many lifetimes from which we learn. In a human lifetime, we can easily see the progression from infant to toddler to child to teenager to young adult and so on. We expect a certain level of maturity based on one's age. Children are supposed to act like children, and adults are supposed to act like adults. We feel we have a standard to use for evaluation.

However, someone's level of spiritual evolution has nothing to do with their physical age in any one lifetime. We may know a person's biological age, but we do not know their spiritual age. They may be relatively new to the planet (and the experiment) and have been through only tens of thousands of lifetimes, or they may have been here since the beginning and have been through hundreds of thousands of lifetimes. A human child may be much farther up the staircase of spiritual evolution than an adult of sixty or seventy. Yet, we expect the sixty-year-old to be more spiritually evolved and responsible than the child. It isn't necessarily so.

This understanding helps us move past judgment into accepting where we are in our process, into allowing and detaching from what others think, feel, say and do, and seeing everyone as a child of Source. If you are aware of where you and others are in the natural flow of evolution, you can more easily allow the process of growing up to take its course.

Spiritual Infancy

Our spiritual infancy begins when we first awaken as spiritual beings and actively begin to pursue our spiritual path. At this stage, we are like little children asking mommy and daddy endless questions, not wanting to miss anything as we look with awe and wonder at the incredible world that has just opened to us. We seek knowledge and soak it up like a sponge, but our understanding is still quite limited because we are still infants in this new world with so much yet to learn.

We are energetic and playful at this stage, just like human children. Everything is new and exciting. Standing in the light for the first time in our meditations is exhilarating and joyful, as it should be. Everything seems easy, and we can't wait for the next steps.

Many members of humanity have not reached the stage of spiritual infancy because they are at the back of the conga line. They are in spiritual preschool and are not yet capable of seeing themselves or others as spiritual beings. This perception will change as the conga line moves forward and those at the back begin to climb the staircase. Until then, we are each to look at ourselves and others with love, compassion, and patience and complete the process of growing up.

Spiritual Adolescence

Our spiritual adolescence begins when we have learned enough to start standing on our own. We start to realize that spiritual growth comes with making choices for ourselves and taking responsibility. We know that Mom and Dad are not always going to be able to take care of us, so we have to begin to learn how to do things on our own. We have to start growing up on a larger scale.

In spiritual adolescence, we are like any human teenager, longing to be grown up and thinking we know it all. We want to stand on our own, show everyone how much we have learned, and prove how grown up we are. Teenagers do not understand that while they have gained a great deal of knowledge, they lack the wisdom that can only be acquired through experience to use that knowledge well. Spiritual adolescents tend to get puffed up, just as human teenagers can during this growth cycle.

Spiritual adolescents cling to what we call spiritual one-liners. Spiritual one-liners are statements of spiritual truth that get tossed around without fully understanding their true meaning. Some of the basic spiritual one-liners are:

- I need to speak my truth
- Everything I need to know is inside me
- All I need to do is love

All these statements are true; however, they each have lower and higher frequency meanings. Spiritual adolescents believe they are standing in their power and walking the talk, but an adolescent does not yet have the higher frequency understanding or wisdom of a master to walk their true path.

A technique used by the Hindu masters is to sit students in front of a verse of the sacred text and have them read it for as long as it takes them to get the next higher octave of understanding. These masters know that spiritual adolescents will go through many levels of comprehension before fully understanding and living the simplicity of divine truth.

Spiritual adolescents often fall into what is known as spiritual significance: "I have all the answers, and my way is the best way." Because adolescents believe they have all the answers, they believe they are helpful as they share their great expanse of knowledge, as in the use of spiritual one-liners. But, as with all teenagers, they don't know what they don't know.

This is a natural part of growing up and is expected in spiritual evolution, just like in human evolution. We need to recognize this phase in our growth, laugh at ourselves when we find ourselves in this space, and resolve to learn our lessons, grow up and move on.

The opposite of spiritual significance is also a pitfall. Often an adolescent withdraws in fear of being judged as too different. Lacking confidence, spiritual teenagers can hide the truth of who they are in fear of losing their status with family and friends. The need to belong to the group and feel safe in what they have known is too great for them to step out and be seen as who they are. This fear will be overcome with time. The courage to allow the beautiful light within to shine will eventually move the fearful adolescent into adulthood.

Adolescence is an essential phase of our spiritual evolution, just as it is in our human evolution. Teenagers are moving out of dependence on their parents, learning how to spread their wings, think for themselves, and make their own decisions. We must honor this phase of our growth and yet be willing to acknowledge its limitations.

We begin the transition into spiritual adulthood when we recognize our spiritual adolescence for what it is, we no longer allow ourselves to be stuck in what we thought was true, and we allow ourselves to grow into higher levels of understanding of divine truth. We must be willing to change what we believe as we move through our various levels of spiritual evolution.

Spiritual Maturity

Our spiritual maturity begins as we gain the experience that gives us the wisdom that moves us out of our adolescence. One fundamental energy here is humility. In spiritual maturity, we realize how much we do not know and are wise enough to slow down, discern, and change our truth.

The spiritual adult no longer holds on to that which does not serve. The spiritual adult neither needs nor desires to impress others because they focus on inner evolution—the outer world is unimportant. In spiritual maturity, we no longer need to impose our truth on others but are confident enough in our truth to share our beliefs without fear or apology when called upon to do so.

In spiritual infancy, we are just *so* excited. We tend to babble with that excitement about what we have learned, often astounded that others are not as excited as we are. We don't know what we don't know yet, so we just pour it out. In spiritual adolescence, we either expound with arrogance all that we have learned and go into judgment of those who do not get it, or we shrink into ourselves in fear of being judged as different and being found unfit.

In spiritual maturity, we are neither in fear nor arrogance. Humility has become the basis for understanding our process and seeing ourselves in the world. We are detaching more and more from the outer illusion and going further and further inward to the experience of ourselves as Source. We no longer judge what others think about us because we have a stronger sense of self-esteem and inner knowing. We no longer need to defend ourselves as we did in spiritual adolescence. We can discern what serves us and what does not. We feel whole and complete. We have finally grown up.

Spiritual adults have no judgment about the stages of evolution. Spiritual adults also understand that physical age has nothing to do with spiritual maturity and are perfectly all right with this. I have met fifteen-year-old spiritual masters and seventy-year-old spiritual infants. It is just their position in the conga line.

Divine Innocence

While moving from spiritual infancy to spiritual maturity, we need to maintain our divine innocence and our childlike nature—childlike, not childish. Many people I meet in my classes have rigid beliefs about the behavior of a "spiritual master." Many believe that spiritual pursuits are always stoic in their seriousness and that spiritual masters have no sense of humor. The opposite is the truth.

True masters are filled with joy that reflects in all areas of their lives. This light-heartedness does not mean that they do not take their spirituality seriously. Their entire life purpose is spiritual evolution and transcending the illusion of this world. However, when you see and feel the divine love of oneness, how can you not want to smile and share that joy?

The teaching of Master Jesus in *1st Corinthians* is often misunderstood and interpreted to demand a serious and solemn demeanor for those dedicated to their spiritual path. Jesus said, "When I was a child, I spoke like a child, I thought like a child, I reasoned like a child; when I became an adult, I put an end to childish ways."[13]

Growing up *does* mean having to give up our childish behaviors and views of the world. However, growing up does *not* mean giving up our youthful joy, laughter, and playfulness. Remember that Jesus also said,

---

[13] 1st Corinthians 13:11, *NRSV Bible with the Apocrypha*, Kindle Edition, HarperCollins, New York, NY, 2011.

"Truly I tell you, unless you change and become like children, you will never enter the kingdom of heaven."[14] Jesus was referring to the importance of divine innocence, an attribute of a true master.

Innocence has many 3rd dimensional meanings. Two of those definitions that are important to understanding divine innocence are:

- A lack of worldly experience or sophistication, a lack of knowledge.
- Freedom from guilt or sin through being unacquainted with evil.[15]

The human lower-self wants and needs to look good, informed, competent, and successful. The lower-self does not want to look unworldly, unknowing, naïve, or unsophisticated. The soul could not care less about those outer world appearances. The more open you are to the lack of experience, the more open you are to new experiences. The more open you are to not knowing everything, the more open you are to learning. Lack of experience, sophistication, and knowledge are good things on the road to spiritual growth.

The lower-self wants freedom and unlimitedness, yet cloaks itself in guilt, shame, regret, and more because it believes in wrongdoing and evil. Young children do not see themselves as bad or wrong until others tell them they are. This perception goes back to understanding and viewing everything in terms of frequency versus right and wrong.

I am not saying that children do not need direction and correction. They do. However, parents, teachers, and society need to take a new look at how we give guidance and discipline to children and ourselves. When we can view ourselves and others with love and compassion instead of judgment, we have a greater chance of viewing ourselves as only out of alignment instead of bad or evil. When we see our lessons as learning opportunities, whether our behavior is loving or not, we have a greater chance of integrating the higher frequency behavior because we become educated on why we do what we do.

---

[14] Matthew 18:3, *NRSV Bible with the Apocrypha*, Kindle Edition, HarperCollins, New York, NY, 2011.

[15] *Random House Webster's College Dictionary*, Random House, Inc., New York, NY, 1991.

Imagine evaluating each life experience that is unloving as, "Oops, I need to do better next time," instead of condemnation. Imagine experiencing every "oops" in life as just another lesson to be learned...no guilt, shame, or regret. This attitude is divine innocence. It is the joy of being a child that is loved.

I know this sounds very simplistic to those challenged as parents and teachers, but it is a starting point—a change in how most people view teaching and disciplining children. This change includes the way we talk to ourselves. No one will say that the transition will be easy, but the way ascended masters speak to us is how we need to begin speaking to all others.

I had a student relay something she had observed in a department store. The mother of a young child, probably two years old, was involved with a clerk when she heard glass shattering. The youngster, who was three-years-old, had picked up a glass ball from a display and dropped it on the floor, where it had shattered. My student expected the mother to explode. Instead, the mom turned around and saw the wide-eyed expression on her child's face and said, "I bet you thought that ball was going to bounce, didn't you?" Instead of scolding the child, she taught the child and paid for the glass ball. My student learned a valuable lesson about how our souls teach us when we are willing to focus on the lessons instead of the "oops."

Joy, laughter, and playfulness are qualities of spiritual masters and are important for anyone on the road to Ascension. Masters are in awe and wonder at the unfolding of creation and are fascinated by human behavior and choices. Masters are free of the judgments and inhibitions of the 3rd dimension and revel in the joy of life. My friend Kris said, "One is never too old to be a child of God." Have fun on your road to Ascension. Learn to be a kid again and enjoy the journey.

Only Keep What Serves

Our truth fluctuates depending on our level of consciousness. It is up to us to discern what is our truth and what is not at any point in time. This change in our beliefs is a necessary and appropriate aspect of our evolution. New "truth" is essential for our mastery. A first-grader learns and believes one version of history at age six, but learns another version in high school and yet another in college. Likewise, as a spiritual student, you will travel through a series of teachings and higher frequency understandings of those teachings on your spiritual journey. One of my favorite Buddhist parables is the man and the raft.

> The Buddha began: "A man is trapped on one side of a fast-flowing river. Where he stands, there is great danger and uncertainty—but on the far side of the river, there is safety.
>
> "Yet there is no bridge or ferry for crossing. So the man gathers logs, leaves, and vines and fashions them together in a raft, sturdy enough to carry him. By lying on the raft and using his arms to paddle, he crosses the river to safety."
>
> The Buddha then asks the listeners a question: "What would you think if the man, having crossed over the river, then said to himself, 'Oh, this raft has served me so well, I should strap it on to my back and carry it overland now'?"
>
> The monks replied that it would not be very sensible to cling to the raft in such a way.
>
> The Buddha continues: "What if he lay the raft down gratefully, thinking that this raft has served him well but is no longer of use and can thus be left upon the shore?"
>
> The monks replied that this would be the proper attitude.
>
> The Buddha concluded by saying: "So it is with my teachings, which are like a raft, and are for crossing over with — not for seizing hold of."

Changing Beliefs

Changing your beliefs can be scary because it means changing your reality—changing your truth about the way things are. Yet, as your frequency goes higher, consciousness begins to shift, and your beliefs must change to match the new frequency. The fear of surrendering the old reality for a new one stops some people cold on their way back to oneness. It is not always easy to move up the ladder of understanding and accept multiple levels of truth. Spiritual evolution requires courage and conviction.

It would seem that we could just make a wish, set an intention, and quickly remember. While that is possible, it is not the norm. We came into the experiment in separation one step at a time, and we were designed to exit the experiment one step at a time. Those who have had "spontaneous awakenings" often find it difficult to integrate and balance after such an influx of energy. It certainly has been done and still can be. However, being the tortoise instead of the hare will be the easier and most productive path for many.

Some years ago, I met a man who shared a theory he called *the scientific basis of change*. I do not remember where he heard this, so I will repeat the theory as I understand it. People generally hold on to a belief until something proves that belief to be wrong. People are willing to change their beliefs when they have enough proof to support the change. They then hold on to the new belief until something else comes along to prove that belief wrong, and so forth.

This process is reflected in many things human beings *knew* to be correct but changed. The earth was the center of the solar system until Copernicus and Galileo proved it differently. The world was flat for Europeans until Columbus sailed to the New World. The four-minute mile was impossible until Roger Bannister proved it was not. A man could never fly to the moon until someone did. Human history is full of stories that demonstrate the scientific basis of change.

However, all changes of belief do not come from dramatic demonstrations of proof. We do not always have to be hit on the head to shift. Every day, people change their beliefs based on life experiences and observations. Recognizing that something is not working and needs to change is a change in your belief system. Going through an experience that changes how you see the world is a change in your truth.

Spiritual evolution often requires accepting new beliefs without proof. Because the physical world is an illusion, giving physical proof for higher spiritual principles is often impossible. One just knows in their heart that something is true. The inner knowing is so strong that their beliefs must change to match that feeling. Once the new beliefs are accepted, life is never the same.

Going back to the pyramids of consciousness, the 3rd and 5th-dimensional levels of consciousness are opposites.

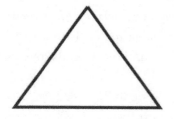

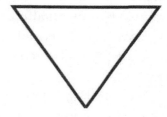

3-D Consciousness **5-D Consciousness**

I tell my students to expect to learn that everything they have believed to be true is false because everything inside the experiment is the opposite of everything outside of it. Nothing in the 3rd dimension is real. Everything in the 5th dimension is. Third-dimensional consciousness is based on separation, ego-gratification, fear, and need. Fifth-dimensional consciousness is based on unity and oneness for the highest good of all, trust, and unlimitedness. One cannot hold on to the old way of being and move into the 5th dimension.

For example, justice in the 3rd dimension is righting a wrong, making things even, punishment and retribution. Justice in the 5th dimension merely brings everyone and everything back into unity and oneness with divine forgiveness and love. In the 3rd dimension, actions are seen as right or wrong and should have the appropriate outcomes. In the 5th dimension, actions are observed as experiences of separation that need to be healed and brought back into unity and oneness; there is no judgment. These versions of justice are energetic opposites.

As our frequency goes higher, we gradually understand the higher meaning in the spiritual one-liners and divine truth. We move from our 3rd-

dimensional understanding to our 4th to our 5th. But, if one's truth is constantly changing, which truth is correct? They all are.

Our Truth

At lower levels of consciousness, we believe there is only one truth. We believe in absolute rights and wrongs. As we begin to mature, we understand that everyone has their truth based on their experiences and where they are in their evolution.

As of this writing, we have more than seven billion people on the planet, and each one of them has their personal beliefs, which means we have more than seven billion versions of the truth. One is not right, and one is not wrong. They are different because of cultural heritage, education, religious teachings, and other factors.

We generally believe what we have been taught is true. However, what someone raised in the United States is taught to believe is true will be different from what someone raised in Canada, Mexico, Honduras, Great Britain, China, Taiwan, or any other country is taught to believe is true. This concept applies across all cultures, all religions, and all nations. One set of beliefs does not make all others invalid, just different.

Reconciling the idea that there are many valid truths is challenging for most people. Most people believe in a strict right and wrong and tend to judge what is different from their beliefs. Yet every culture has its views and ways of doing things, making the world a fascinating place.

Your spiritual beliefs are no different than your other beliefs. You need to be tolerant of the many opinions and approaches to who you are as a spiritual being. You will end up in oneness no matter what path you take, so be patient with yourself and others, and allow change to take its own pace. All there is, is love.

Multidimensional Beings

We exist at many levels, or dimensions, of consciousness. We have a certain level of evolution that can be achieved while we are in a human body. As our frequency increases, we have no choice but to eventually let go of the human form if we are to continue to evolve. That is no different from graduating high school and moving on to the next phase of life. It is just another stage of growing up.

Just as we are supposed to go out into the world after our schooling to get jobs and be part of the larger society, we are supposed to go higher in frequency and ascend. Leaving the body behind is an exciting part of the graduation process, but can only happen in the state of divine oneness.

Not only must you be one with All That Is around you, but you must also be one with all *you* are. Think of yourself as a Yoyo. In the larger sense of who you are, your hand is your self-as-Source, and the Yoyo is what you know as your human self, your lower-self. For you to descend into the experiment, your soul released the Yoyo and decreased your frequency until the string on the Yoyo was extended entirely, and you believed yourself to be human. Each inch of the Yoyo string is an aspect of you existing at a higher frequency, a higher level of consciousness, between your lower-self and your soul. You are a multi-dimensional being and exist at many levels of consciousness, all at the same time. In a way, you are your own conga line.

You have never been separate from the string between your lower-self and your soul. Each inch of the string is you, and you are each inch of the string. As your frequency moves higher, you move back up the line toward reunion with your soul. As you make this journey, you merge into the next higher level of consciousness of who you are as Source. All parts of you are becoming one.

At the lower levels of consciousness, we view the soul as something outside ourselves, something separate from who we are. That has never been true. Until we heal and feel one within ourselves, we cannot feel one with others or with Source.

The upper dimensions of ourselves guide us and help us prepare for Ascension when we allow ourselves to listen and trust. The upper dimensions of ourselves see and know what we do not. We merely have to trust.

Instead of thinking of yourself as a Yoyo, now think of yourself as a skyscraper. The lower-self sits on the first floor. The next higher dimension of yourself sits on the second floor, and so on, until you reach the penthouse, where your soul resides. There are an unlimited number of floors between you and your soul, so you can insert as many floors as you like.

Your lower-self can only acquire limited information when you look out the window from the first floor. From this point of view, you have too many obstacles to seeing very far down either side of the street.

However, the part of you that sits on the ninth floor of your skyscraper has a much better view. All you have to do is call up and ask for more information. Each higher floor in your skyscraper has a better view and access to more information than the one below it. Your soul, which sits in the penthouse, has a 360° view and access to everything you need to know. All you have to do is ask!

Learning to connect clearly and channel to your self-as-Source is essential to knowing what is in your highest good at any time. Your fastest and easiest way home is to learn to access and follow your guidance. The critical piece is learning to be 100% connected and clear.

We Each Have the Choice

One of my favorite hiking trails in the eastern part of the United States is the Rich Mountain Trail in Moses Cone Memorial Park in the Blue Ridge Mountains. The Moses Cone estate offers twenty-five miles of old carriage trails for hiking.

The Rich Mountain Trail follows an old road that circles several times around a lovely domed mountain as it climbs to where a carriage house used to sit. Over the years, energetic hikers have cut a trail straight up the side of the mountain to bypass the loops. Hikers can choose to follow the old road that circles to the top or use the new trail that cuts straight to the top. The old road alternates between open spaces with great views of the Blue Ridge and lovely old forest areas that provide shade and woodland wildlife for those who want a leisurely climb to the top. The new trail has glorious views of the Blue Ridge for the entire climb and offers a great workout for those who want to huff and puff to get to the top faster.

The journey from the start of the trail, point A, to the end of the trail, point B, takes the same amount of energy whether one circles around the mountain or cuts straight up the side. Circling exerts the energy more gradually than chugging quickly up the side. Both paths lead to the top. One is not better than the other, but they offer different experiences with different views and comfort levels.

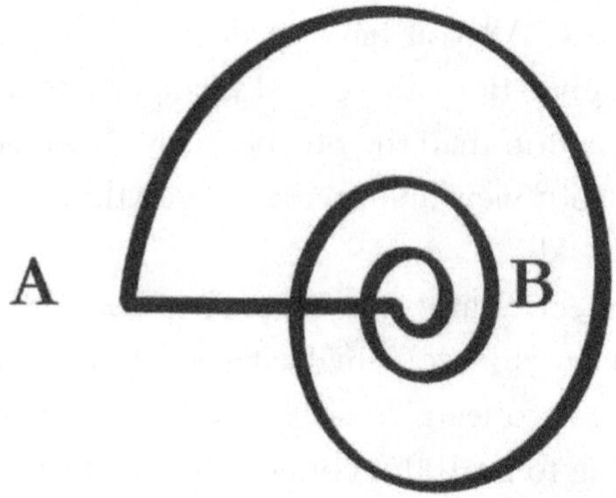

A hiker can even choose a combination of the two trails by making one circuit around the mountain and then taking a portion of the cut-through. Any of the three choices will get a hiker to the top where the old carriage house used to sit.

Our spiritual journey is the same. One can take the slower or the faster path, but one will get to the top all the same. The important point is that both paths require the same amount of energy.

Going again to the book *What is Lightbody*, in which Arial explains the variety of changes the human body goes through during ascension and what we can expect as the symptoms of moving into the light, Arial says that we each have a choice of how we experience the change. We can move slowly and allow the physical changes to occur gradually, or we can move quickly and accept the shift with more intensity. It is just a choice, like choosing a path up the mountain. One can choose to move slowly, or one can choose to move quickly. But one must choose to move.[16]

---

[16] Tachi-ren, Tashira and Archangel Ariel, *What is Lightbody,* World Tree Press, Payson, AZ, 1999.

Let Change Be Easy

Growing up and allowing change does not have to be difficult, but human beings tend to make it so. Change is as simple as holding a clear intention to accept change for the highest good and allowing oneself to accept it.

As I have said before, *simple* does not mean *easy*. However, the only reason change is not easy is that we are afraid to let go.

The ability to make changes quickly as we move into our light is easier now than it has ever been on this planet. Change will still be challenging. Human beings are quite attached to the past and how things have been, but the planet itself is rapidly shifting and moving into higher levels of light, which means humanity must follow.

An example of how rapidly change can occur is the Harmonic Convergence of August 1987. In 1987, humanity was about to fall off the cliff. The doom and gloom prophecies of ancient times were about to catch up to us, and we appeared to be in a hopeless downhill spiral. The Spiritual Hierarchy sent the word out through many channels around the world for people to gather during the days of the Harmonic Convergence to create a massive shift in human consciousness.

A harmonic convergence is a rare alignment of the sun, moon, and planets of our solar system that is said to open unique portals for shifting energy. The Harmonic Convergence of 1987 was special.

People were guided to meditate on their own or create group meditations to focus light and love on humanity on August 16th and 17th of that year to take advantage of the energy of the Harmonic Convergence. Many people traveled to sacred sites such as Machu Picchu, Mt. Shasta, and Giza to partake in gatherings to help change the course of humanity.

I was not a member of these awakened human beings. I was still sleeping soundly in the darkness and oblivious to all that was happening in the metaphysical world. However, I am profoundly grateful to those who were awake at the time. I now know through personal channelings where humanity would have found themselves if not for the efforts of a small number of human beings who understood how to use their intentions of love to create change.

Because of the actions taken during the Harmonic Convergence and the efforts of many others since then, Mother Earth and humanity are moving quickly and creating significant change. As the overall frequency of Mother Earth and humankind goes higher, every human being has the chance to make the shift toward unconditional love easier.

When we look at the turmoil on the planet now, we could wonder how this is true. The discord and upheavals we see now around the world are the symptoms of increasing light. The lower frequencies find it difficult to maintain their power and act out in anger and rage at the fear of losing what they believe should be theirs. This, too, shall pass. Remain focused on love and remember how the efforts of a few who understand can change the course of an entire planet.

Because of the higher frequency of the planet, the healing process for humanity has moved from 95/5% to 97/3% to 98/2%—which I am about to explain. In the not-too-distant future, it will be even easier to make the change.

The Ninety-Eight and Two

Before I met Kris, I had encountered the healing numbers 97% and 3% in two sets of teachings. The teachers who shared this information with me had learned in their channelings that their work would help people heal 97% of their issues. However, neither of these teachers knew what the other 3% was.

When I met Kris, she had also received the 97% and 3% figures in her channelings; only she understood the last 3%. At that time, most of what humans needed to heal (the 97%) could be remedied simply by raising the frequency high enough to allow the transformation. Healing techniques range from meditation to chanting to Reiki or other energy practices.

However, everyone has issues of judgments and personal denials that need to come to their awareness to be healed. In other words, everyone needs to come into a minimal level of self-awareness, or self-realization, to heal completely for Ascension. These issues were the last 3%.

As time goes on and the frequency of humanity as a whole gets higher, the amount of healing that can be done simply by "standing in the light" until the frequency is high enough to create change gets larger. It truly is getting easier for humanity to heal its issues. The following is an excerpt from a channeling I received from the Spiritual Hierarchy in August 2013.

Beloveds —

A few short weeks ago, humanity passed an important milestone in its evolution. For many decades, the people of this planet have been clearing through what We have called the 97% and 3%. This meant 97% of human issues could be cleared simply by standing in the White Light, doing resonances, running energy, meditation, etc. However, 3% of one's issues needed to come to conscious awareness for healing to achieve self-realization and understanding. For many decades prior to the 97% and 3%, the clearing standard was 95% and 5%. Through the diligent efforts of spiritual students and teachers during those decades, the standard was raised to 97% and 3%.

Now, through the wonderful work of so many, the clearing standard for all of humanity, not just those who have been consciously on their paths but for all, is now 98% and 2%. Many of you have already reached a level of self-awareness such that little needs to come to your conscious awareness for healing. We are so very, very pleased.

In time, much less time than you may imagine, the standard will rise to 99% and 1%, and eventually, people will be able to shift so quickly that instant christ consciousness will be attainable. This has not yet occurred, so stay the course of your chosen studies and follow your guidance. Your soul knows which path will serve you best. There are many roads to the Buddha and will always be.

These are very exciting times for everyone. We have said this to you often, but now We hope you are truly beginning to see and feel that the end is near. You are so close to being home.

MAY YOU FEEL THE LOVE OF SOURCE WITHIN YOU ALWAYS,
The Spiritual Hierarchy

Choosing to Change Is Choosing to Evolve

When you look at the upheaval in the world, you may find it difficult to believe that it is as simple as the 98% and the 2%, but it is. Allowing the 98% to heal by using high-frequency transformation techniques is not only simple, but it also feels wonderful. Allowing yourself to fill with and feel the love of Source is bliss. You just have to choose to do it.

Looking at the 2% is more challenging because we rarely want to look at what we judge, but it is only 2%. Once you have identified an issue that has been denied, healing it is as simple as healing the 98%. You just let in enough love using the same techniques.

None of this happens overnight. Consistent daily meditation and energy techniques are necessary and easy to do. You must select a road to the Buddha and follow it. Yes, it means dedication and commitment. Yes, it means discipline. But, the rewards of the exaltation of the experience of oneness are beyond words and human experience.

Consider everything you do daily to meet the needs of a 3rd-dimensional life. You shower, eat and drink, brush your teeth, and so on. To meet your spiritual needs, you must meet the needs of a 5th-dimensional life. That means adding spiritual practices to your daily routine and continuing those practices until only the joy of your connection to your soul is all-important. As a friend once said: lather, rinse, repeat, lather, rinse, repeat. That is all that it takes to get to oneness and Ascension.

Humanity is closer than most realize to making a giant leap toward unity and oneness. When you make a choice to grow up as a spiritual being and choose a path to Ascension, living in unity and oneness is just around the corner. However, we still have much to learn about the differences between living in a 3rd-dimensional community and a 5th-dimensional community.

Chapter 6

Living in Unity

Truly I tell you, just as you did it to one of the least of these who are members of my family, you did it to me.
—Matthew 25:40, *The NRSV Bible*

In most, if not all, of our spiritual evolution, one lesson must be learned and mastered before moving on to the next. While many lessons will overlap to attain ultimate mastery, a full understanding of one lesson leads to a full understanding of the one to follow. Unity and oneness are two of those lessons. Unity with all things must be achieved before fully knowing divine oneness.

Many people view Ascension as the ticket out of here, as I did when I first began my spiritual quest. For those people, the goal is to get out of human form and off the planet as quickly as possible. They do not feel comfortable with the density around them and see *out there* as better than here. Some even wear spiritual martyrdom's earthly pain and suffering as a badge of courage.

Ascension is about re-creating the concept *and* the experience of heaven on earth. Ascension is about moving through and healing all judgment and all fear. It is about learning that no place is better than here, no matter where here is.

We all need to understand that it is not what we want but why we want it. Kris simplified this teaching: "It is not the what, it is the why." This truth applies to everything. It is not what you do but why you do it. It is not what you say but why you say it. It is not what you believe but why you believe it.

Ascension is not a question of wanting to graduate from life on earth. The question is why you want to graduate from life on earth. As long as you hold judgment or fear of the experience here, you are not in unconditional love and heaven on earth. Without these, there is no graduation.

Heaven is a state of being, not a location. It is an experience, not a destination. The heavenly state exists in our hearts and must be projected from there into the outer reality in every moment of every day. It is only in the state of divine love and grace, free of all judgment, that one is ready to ascend.

One of the great paradoxes of spiritual evolution is that until you love it here on Earth so much you no longer desire to leave, you get to stay until you do. When you understand and accept the purpose of being here and are free of all judgment, you are ready to go. Until then, you go around and around.

Re-creating the concept of heaven on earth is about re-creating divine community on earth—a community that operates at 5th-dimensional consciousness. Divine community, often called christed community, is based on unconditional love.

If you are holding any judgment of any kind, you are not in unconditional love and, therefore, are not in unity and oneness. If you are not in unity and oneness with All That Is, you are not in the complete experience of yourself as Source. There is no way around this. As long as you desire to get out of here, you are missing the point of why you came. It is all about, and only about, love and freedom from all judgments.

The Steps to Oneness

The 3rd dimension defines oneness as *being a single unit with a single identity and a single mind.*[17] While I will take the definition of divine oneness further later, it is a good starting point as it is the foundation of a spiritual community and the way out of the illusion. A spiritual community cannot exist as people living together for security and support with like-minded people but still wanting to maintain a layer of separation and individuality. There must be a single unified identity, and a single unified mind for a community to exist at the christed-level. The unified identity and unified mind do not take away our uniqueness or specialness. However, they dissolve our separation from each other and eliminate the lower-self's need for individuality, drive to be different, and desire for self-gratification.

We cannot reach a state of divine oneness without first reaching a state of divine unity. We cannot achieve a state of unity without first achieving harmony and cooperation. The energetic progression from harmony to cooperation to unity to oneness is mastered in stages. We cannot skip the steps.

Divine Harmony and Cooperation

In the *I AM Presence* series, Saint Germaine teaches that one must master divine love, peace, and harmony to ascend to the next dimension.[18] I agree wholeheartedly.

Harmony is the key to the effortless flow we all seek. This effortless flow cannot just be on an individual basis for a community to exist in unity and oneness. It must be present for all members of a divine community.

Divine harmony means working together, free of conflict or discord. Divine harmony is free of guilt, shame, or blame. Instead, it is love, patience, and peace in the process of creation and evolution. Harmony opens the heart and the mind to new opportunities and expands your universe.

---

17 *Random House Webster's College Dictionary*, Random House, Inc., New York, NY, 1991.

18 King, Godfré Ray, *Unveiled Mysteries,* Saint Germain Series, Vol. 1, 4th edition, Saint Germain Press, 1989.

While peace helps create harmony, harmony also helps create a greater sense of peace. The effortless flow of harmony allows cooperation.

Divine cooperation is thinking and acting in harmony with others for the common good or shared benefit. Divine cooperation is free of competition and the desire for personal gain. In a divine community, everyone works together for the mutual benefit of the whole. Everyone's needs are considered, and everyone's needs are met.

The concept is simple, but not easy for humanity to achieve. This level of cooperation means surrendering the little will (what I think is good for me) to Divine Will (what I know is good for the whole). While the highest good of the whole is always in the highest good of the parts, the lower-self often sees it as a personal sacrifice.

In the 3rd-dimensional paradigm, you can fake harmony and cooperation for personal gain to make a profit, to look good, or to be accepted by others. In the 3rd-dimensional paradigm, you can appear to work in harmony and cooperation in the outer world without necessarily having harmony and cooperation as the true inner motivations. This behavior is easily understood by watching a talented con-man and has given rise to the phrase "a wolf in sheep's clothing."

In the 5th-dimensional paradigm, you cannot fake it, nor do you want to fake it. In the 5th-dimensional paradigm, motivation is always for the highest good of all and the spiritual evolution of everyone in the community.

Shirley MacLaine explained this concept beautifully in her book, *The Camino: A Journey of the Spirit*, when she wrote about her experiences in Lemuria. Ms. MacLaine described memories of meditation circles devoted to raising the frequency and consciousness of everyone in the circle. The focus was always on everyone's evolution.[19]

In a divine community, a 5th-dimensional community, only the inner world matters because the outer world is understood to be an illusion. The inner reaction, the inner feeling, is the test of where you are in your evolution, not how you act on the outer. Outer world actions can be faked. Outer

---

[19] MacLaine, Shirley, *The Camino: A Journey of the Spirit*, Pocket Books/Division of Simon & Schuster, Inc., New York, NY, 2000.

world actions are an indication of where you might be, but not necessarily of where you are. The truth always lies in the heart.

You must *be* harmony and cooperation. You must vibrate with these energies to truly master them. Only in the mastery of the higher frequencies will you find your self-as-Source. You begin by doing harmony and cooperation to the best of your ability in the outer world. However, you must eventually become these energies if you are to move into the level of unity that will lead you into oneness. In other words, act as if you are there until you are there. Or, as some say, fake it till you make it.

The Shift to Divine Power

Moving into divine harmony and cooperation also means shifting into divine power—the power of your self-as-Source versus the power of your lower-self. This shift is one of the most significant changes you must make to realize yourself as Source.

The power of the lower-self, the power of 3rd-dimensional consciousness, is using your power over others for self-serving means. At this level, you use your energy to get what you want without necessarily considering or caring about the effect on others. It is all about you.

Third-dimensional power can be used overtly, as in physical aggression, war, or other obvious behavior, to dominate another. Third-dimensional power can also be used subtly and deviously behind the scenes as verbal, emotional, or mental manipulation. Guilt, shame, praise, and the full range of human emotions have been used to manipulate others into what one desires. This more subtle use of power is as much out of alignment with love as is war or physical domination. The abuse of power is the abuse of power, regardless of its form.

Divine power is using your will through love and wisdom for the highest good of all. It opens your heart to know that we are one and that as you do unto another, so you do unto yourself. Divine power comes from the soul and requires surrender to the Divine Plan regardless of personal gain or loss. This concept is not so easy for the lower-self to grasp. However, it is the foundation of every spiritual path to Ascension, as in, "Thy will, not my will, be done."

Divine power comes with the experience of sovereignty. Sovereignty is an inner knowing of needing no one and no thing from outside yourself to feel whole and complete, no one and no thing outside yourself to feel loved, no one and no thing outside yourself to feel powerful. Third-dimensional power comes from outside. Fifth-dimensional power comes from within. Through the experience of your divine power, you come into unity and, eventually, into oneness.

The journey from 3rd-dimensional to 5th-dimensional power is long, with many layers of evolution and learning. The shift of consciousness in how we use our energy and will is a major part of our 4th-dimensional transformation and an essential part of knowing ourselves as Source.

When everyone in a community operates from divine power by trusting their guidance for the highest good of all, the community flows in harmony and cooperation. Everyone contributes, everyone's voice is heard, no one feels left out or ignored, and an extraordinary level of peace can exist. The lower-self may not always like what is asked of it, but it knows that it is right because it is for the highest good of the whole. When everyone comes from clear guidance, the Divine Plan flows effortlessly, and everyone is abundant. Living in harmony and cooperation allows everyone in a community to thrive and evolve. Eventually, everyone desires only the highest plan.

From Separation into Unity

Harmony and cooperation are the first steps. Taking the next step into unity is a greater challenge. Stepping into unity happens when the lower-self moves from the fear that it might not get what it wants to the fear of losing its identity and individuality completely.

You are here to remember who you are as light. When you awaken and commit to expanding the light within, you are known as a lightworker. As we lightworkers strive to experience ourselves as Source, the concepts of harmony and cooperation are heart-opening. We want to live in peace, harmony, and flow. The movement into unity takes a much higher level of surrender and commitment.

As I have shared, one of the challenges of conveying higher-frequency concepts is the lack of words in the English language to express subtle differences in how the lower-self views and understands certain concepts versus how the soul understands them. Going again to the dictionary, the definitions of unity and oneness are very similar. They even overlap. However, in spiritual studies, unity and oneness have separate definitions and energies that are important for understanding the progression of our evolution.

I define divine unity as *the combination of individual parts into one unit which operates without diversity, unvaried, and uniform in character. The unit operates in solidarity, holding a single thought, a single feeling, a single value. All parts are working for a single cause.*

On the surface, this does not seem like a big deal. In the 3rd dimension, we are familiar with the concept of working together in teams for a shared vision or cause. Teamwork is a good thing. However, in the 3rd dimension, we can opt out if things aren't going the way we like. We can leave the team, quit the job, or reject the plan if we don't like how things affect us.

Divine unity requires the surrender of what you do and the surrender of who you are to the whole. Unity requires complete surrender of who you have been as a separate entity to be part of the whole. The lower-self has perceived itself as an individual for so long that the concept of moving back into Unity when it no longer has a separate identity is a bit intimidating.

Consider *operating without diversity, unvaried, and uniform in character—holding a single thought, a single feeling, a single value.* The lower-self asks, "What happened to *me* in that definition? What happened to *my* identity? What happened to *my* rights, *my* desires, *my* opinions?" Living in harmony and cooperation with others is one thing, but losing one's identity is a different ballgame. Suddenly, this spiritual evolution stuff does not sound so good.

Now, add to this the other concepts essential to unity—*universal*, having the characteristics of the whole; *univocal*, speaking with one voice; *unified*, to merge into one unit; *unilateral*, done on (and for) one side only. In 3rd-dimensional consciousness, you can understand being in these states for a while for some specific purpose. But for the lower-self to exist in these states 100% of the time feels like giving away its power. How can you be all-powerful and not have the choice to be different? The answer is to embrace your uniqueness instead of your individuality.

Individuality versus Uniqueness

Understanding the difference between individuality and uniqueness makes the shift from *me* to *us* easier for the lower-self. The lower-self fears that unity means everyone will be the same and that no one will have a choice. The lower-self fears that we will be like robots, without personality, controlled and boring, when it is actually the opposite.

Human beings pride themselves on being individuals and being different from each other. While many may want to be like their personal hero, some superstar, or their group of friends, the idea of being just like everyone else is abhorrent. People who want to be like the other members of their group still want their group to be different from other groups. The idea of individuality is very important to human beings.

One may think the desire to be different is a statement of personal identity, but it is a declaration of separation from other people. The need for individuality blocks the ability to find our true selves and merge into oneness with others. Inside the illusion of duality, the lower-self has developed a certain level of safety by not getting too close or being vulnerable. The sense of protection from having a personal identity creates a comfort zone that is not easy to relinquish. The lower-self will even fight to hold on to what it believes is safe in fear of surrendering to the whole.

The fear of loss of identity has been the basis for an untold number of science fiction stories. How often have we seen alien invaders coming to earth to steal our humanity by incorporating us into their species and making us *one* with them? These invaders want to take away what we believe makes us human. It goes beyond slavery to annihilation. Instead of seeing the possibility of peace and harmony resulting from merging into the One, humanity considers this merging to be a death sentence and the end of what makes us unique and special.

I am, of course, not saying that we want alien invaders to come to force us into their way of being. However, we do have to look at our fears of moving from individuality into a unified whole. Without this surrender, we cannot experience our true spiritual nature. We must understand that giving up our individuality does not mean losing our uniqueness and what makes each of us special in this universe.

Each human being is a unique creation. There is nothing in the universe that is exactly like anything else. Even identical twins are not entirely alike. Each has unique characteristics, no matter how identical they may seem. Nothing in creation is exactly like you. Understanding this is very important.

Source does not need or want to create two things exactly alike. Source seeks a variety of experiences from which to grow and expand. We are each a small but essential part of that expansion. Our purpose is to have unique experiences as part of Source and the whole.

We each have unique qualities that identify us but do not separate us. The lower-self has difficulty understanding this because the lower-self focuses on what makes it different from everyone else. The lower-self focuses on what makes it an individual instead of how it fits uniquely into the whole. The lower-self seeks uniqueness as a way to *be* special instead of accepting it *is* special. This part of the game of separation must be healed as soon as possible. Knowing yourself as part of the whole opens you to the power of your self-as-Source.

Pieces of the Puzzle

In its need for attention or to be more than someone else, the lower-self clings to its individuality, creates separation, and only temporary satisfaction. In its need to be special by 3rd-dimensional standards, the lower-self misses the point of being special by divine standards. The divine standards make us truly special. These are the gifts and talents that are our unique contribution to the success of the whole. No one on the planet is you or ever will be.

We are designed to be unique parts of the whole, and the whole is not complete without each of its parts in place. A 10,000-piece jigsaw puzzle is incomplete until piece 10,000 is included. No one piece of the puzzle is more important than another. In a jigsaw puzzle, a portion of the sky cannot be a piece of a bush. A part of a bush cannot be a piece of the sky. All pieces have a place in the puzzle. All pieces are special, and all are important. You are important.

When we pull away from the whole to make our mark on the world, we create separation instead of unity. The same happens if we pull away from the whole to hide who we are from the world. Just as no one is more or less special, and no one is more or less unique, no one is more or less divine. No one is more or less a child of Source. Size, wealth, and other forms of 3rd-dimensional power do not matter in the divine realm. Divine worthiness and divine humility are balanced in a spiritual master.

We must all identify, master, and play our unique and special roles in this puzzle that we have created. Without the unity of all things, we cannot be in a state of oneness. Without the unity of all things, we cannot bring separation and duality to an end. In separation and duality, we falter. In separation and duality, we keep repeating the same mistakes. When we operate in unity, we are unstoppable. In unity, we are Source. When we all remember who we are and every piece of the puzzle is in place, the experiment is over forever.

Unity Within

I have been discussing living in unity as part of a divine community. In Chapter 3, I said that to be one with Source, we must be one within ourselves. All our bodies will heal their separation and move back into one unified field. The membranes that exist between the lower bodies will be removed, or dissolved, so that the physical, emotional, and mental bodies can merge back into one energy body. The unified lower body will then be integrated back into oneness with the spiritual bodies. That unified body will then merge back into oneness with All That Is.

If we understand the teaching "as within, so without," we know we must experience full unity within before we can experience complete unity with others, including Source. Everything starts within.

When people tune into my energy field through clairvoyance or kinesthesis, they often ask how my experience feels. I have no way to describe it. We reach a point when our energetic experiences, our spiritual experiences, have transcended human language. The Eastern traditions may have words for these experiences that we do not have in western languages, but they are just words. The only way to understand the experience is to have the experience.

I remember the first time I experienced myself as simultaneously above and below in a meditation. I knew this would happen, but the experience blew me away. Those who meditate regularly know the feeling of being beyond one's body and connected to the universe. However, the time comes when you have full awareness, full consciousness of being human, and being your self-as-Source simultaneously. I thought I knew what that meant until I experienced it and realized I could not put words to that awareness. It got to be fun when I realized I was experiencing this same awareness outside of meditation—being my lower-self and self-as-Source at the same time in each experience I was having.

This expansion into unity can sometimes feel overpowering but is also so beautiful that you will want to know it again and again if you have not already. This experience is where you find your true self. However, before you start asking to feel everything right now, remember that there is a reason we climb the staircase one step at a time. Follow your guidance, be patient, and your soul will soon blow your mind.

Being of Service

Another aspect of unity is the willingness and desire to be of service in whatever way we are called on to serve. In separation, we focus on taking care of ourselves. In unity, we focus on taking care of the whole. Helping others is not a foreign concept to the lower-self, but service without seeing the reward begs the question, who will take care of me?

In its perception of separation from Source and its power as Source, the lower-self feels limited in its ability to serve its own needs. Therefore, the lower-self looks outside itself to get paid or rewarded in some way for its service. It needs to be sure it can provide for itself. In a divine community, when all members are giving of themselves for the highest good of the whole, everyone is served because the energy keeps circulating. When everyone freely gives time, goods, and services without the need for hoarding for self-protection, the community has an endless supply of all that it needs individually and collectively.

You do not have to worry about rewards when you know your power as Source to create what you need through 5th-dimensional power. You can freely be of service, knowing that your needs will always be met. Think of our guides, angels, and teachers who serve us from the spiritual realms. They do not operate in competition for their highest good. They work in cooperation for *our* highest good, each calling on their particular skills and areas of expertise to work together for the highest plan for our spiritual evolution.

They discuss and agree on the highest plan of action to help us learn what we need to know and be where we need to be, and they do their best to help us on our way. They serve us unconditionally without pay because it is their job, joy, and passion. They serve us unendingly and without reservation, even though they may not be recognized or thanked for their contributions to our evolution. They help even when we do not love them back. They put no price tags on their love or service and no expectations on deeds or accomplishments. They have no loss of joy when we do not get it. They just keep serving the highest good of all.

Our guides, angels, and teachers do not experience separation as we do on earth. They do not worry over their personal needs because they know themselves as one with Source, and, therefore, all-powerful. They do not see themselves as more significant than others, so they do not feel the need to have more than others. They just serve.

This explanation may seem simplistic as we humans still have bodies and the physical world needs that those without bodies do not have. The principles and processes of creating this level of community on earth are a book in themselves. However, go to the temples and ashrams of this planet, and you will see human beings doing their best to master the same experience of community that our guides, angels, and teachers know.

Shifting into unity requires letting go of the old ways of doing things and adopting new ways of working in a community. This change is not easy. The lower-self is reluctant to give up what it perceives as freedom, individuality, property, and safety. It is essential to understand that unity and community do not mean we must give up everything we have.

The concepts of divine abundance, divine reward, and personal expansion are critical to a thriving community. Our divinity is not about poverty or selflessness to the point of self-detriment. Our divinity is in our motivations for what we want and in finding balance. Our perfection is in our non-attachment to the needs of the physical world. This topic is also an entire book in itself. I recommend asking to feel the energy of unity as much and as often as possible. Eventually, the understanding of it will feel clear and exciting.

Surrendering to the Whole

Many people find the concept of surrendering individual needs to the needs of the whole unrealistic. The transition from 3rd-dimensional love (based on self-gratification) to 5th-dimensional Love (based on selflessness) is dramatic.

In 3rd-dimensional consciousness, we seek to fill our needs from the outside because we do not feel whole and complete within. For the lower-self, who lacks sufficient self-love, the need for external power, possessions, position, and self-service is a necessity. We have all either been through or are going through some stage of this now.

In 5th-dimensional consciousness, we seek only to share divine love through the joy of service because our self-love is all we need to feel whole and complete. At this level of self-love, surrendering to the highest good of the whole is easy because we do not need anything from outside ourselves to feel powerful, safe, or loved. All experience becomes selfless as we experience ourselves as Source.

The most incredible experience of love at the 3rd-dimensional level shrinks to nothingness with the knowledge of divine love. Third-dimensional love keeps us in separation as we look to the lower-self's needs first. The shift into 5th-dimensional love moves us step by step through the joy and overwhelming bliss of divine love that leads to unity and oneness with all things.

In a divine community, we work to repair the broken, separated version of love in 3rd-dimensional consciousness. In a divine community, we seek to be in unconditional love, even in the face of great challenges. In unity, we try to the best of our ability to be one with everything at all times. Divine unity means seeing, feeling, and experiencing others as part of ourselves. From that space, we never put the lower-self's needs above the needs of another.

We are generally taught in metaphysical or spiritual studies to ask for what is in our highest good. The Standing in the Light® program recommends always asking for what is in the highest good of all. This distinction is important because the answer to these two questions is not always the same. The majority of the time, it is, but not always.

Believe it or not, there are times when something can be in your highest good but not in the highest good of the whole. However, the highest good of the whole is always in your individual highest good, even if you cannot see it at first. Living in unity requires asking for the highest good of the community. We have no way of knowing what that is from our mental bodies. Only our souls know all the factors involved, which takes us back to trusting and following our guidance.

Some years ago, I was offered a financial opportunity that was very appealing. It involved working with a group of people on a project with high-income potential. These were lovely people with a great idea. When I asked my soul if it was in my highest good to participate, I heard *yes*. However, when I double-checked by asking if it was the highest good of all for me to participate, I heard *no*. Bummer.

I was able to discern that this group needed to learn to do what I would have done for them. While I would have made a nice income working on a valuable project, I would have enabled the group to stand in the shadows instead of stepping into their power. When I declined the offer, they learned what they needed to do on their own to make the project a success.

I had co-created an opportunity to test my resolve to honor the highest good of all above my benefit. It was beautiful to watch the group expand. My gift to myself was the knowledge that I helped facilitate that expansion by surrendering to the highest good of the whole, saying *no,* and letting them soar. I also proceeded to create a new option for myself, which has served me well.

Dependence, Independence, and Interdependence

Part of spiritual evolution is moving from dependence/co-dependence into independence into interdependence. This progression is also important and must be mastered in this order. We cannot master interdependence without mastering independence. It is one of the keys to the experience of divine unity and divine community.

We understand dependence and co-dependence as neediness. These are the need of someone outside of yourself to be all right, feel safe, and be taken care of. Independence is the first big step in finding your ability to be self-sufficient. It is the autonomy that comes with accepting personal choice and taking action on your own without needing someone to do it for you.

Interdependence is a balance of knowing yourself as all-powerful (not *needing* anyone to do it for you) and, at the same time, recognizing that you are an integral part of the community. Everything that you do affects all members of your community. It is the balance of knowing that, as Source, you *can* do it all, yet understanding you are not here to do it all by yourself. We are each a unique piece of the puzzle, and we are here to learn how to allow and coordinate everyone's abilities and efforts. As the old saying goes, do what you do best and let others do the rest. There are reasons why we each came in with different skills.

A successful community can be tricky relative to interdependence. If one has not fully mastered independence, one can easily fall back into dependence/codependence in the guise of community. I'll go back to the story I shared when I was guided not to participate in a very appealing opportunity. Without realizing what they were doing, the people who wanted my help were dropping into dependence on me to do what they could do for themselves. They did not know how to do it and were afraid to try. When I said no, they resolved to learn to do it themselves, and they were great.

We need to know when it is appropriate to ask for help and when it is not. We need to know when it is appropriate to help others and when it is not. A spiritual master is never embarrassed to ask for help and will not say no when guided to assist. The question goes back to it's not the what; it's the why—does the motivation come from true interdependence in the flow of community, or does it come from fear, laziness, or other lower frequency energies? Again, it is simple, but not always easy.

We do not reach interdependence overnight. We learn through our experiences in a community. In a community, we must be able to accept others just as they are and yet require spiritual growth to be part of the community. The spiritual community cannot grow unless all the members are growing. Members of a community will not grow at the same pace or even in the same direction because each is on their own path. However, each member is actively doing their best to become the greatest spiritual being that they can be and supporting others in doing the same.

Unity supports both individual and community growth by creating an environment of unconditional love free of judgments, restrictions, and expectations. All members must feel free to screw up in their learning process without fear of the repercussions or loss of love because, screw up, we will.

Chapter 7

Achieving Oneness

All things share the same breath - the beast, the tree, the man, the air shares its spirit with all the life it supports.
—Chief Seattle

We are all one. You have heard this over and over, but what does it mean? If we are all one, what does that feel like, and how many people have ever truly experienced divine oneness?

To understand oneness, first, consider prime numbers. A prime number can only be divided by itself and 1…3-5-7-11-13-17, etc. When a prime number is divided by itself, we get 1. When a prime number is divided by 1, we get the prime number itself. 3÷3=1. 3÷1=3. In the world of number 3, only number 1 and it exists.

As one with Source, you can only be divided by yourself and Source. Source divided by you is still Source and you divided by Source is still you. In other words, you cannot be separate from the oneness of all things. You cannot be separate from Source. You can only believe and perceive that you have been.

You are *divine prime.* In your universe, only Source and you exist. Everything around you is part of the illusion you are creating and co-creating for your evolution. You are divine oneness with all things, whether you are experiencing it yet or not. It cannot be otherwise.

Divine oneness is the foundation of the principle of mirrors. Every great spiritual path teaches that we are mirrors of each other. We cannot see something in another person unless it is a part of us; therefore, everyone we see is a reflection of who we are at any one point in time.

In my universe, only Source and I exist. Everyone I am creating and co-creating in my universe is a reflection of how I see Source and how I see myself. It cannot be otherwise because, in divine oneness, I am also divine prime. I am not divisible from the world around me. I am creating my experiences for my evolution. If I pay attention and accept what I am creating, I see and know myself as one with All That Is. If I do not accept responsibility and blame others instead, I perceive separation, especially if I blame Source.

The principle of mirrors is challenging for most of us when we first get started. We have believed ourselves to be victims for so long that the concept that everyone else reflects who we are is not just hard to grasp; it is hard to swallow when we do not like the mirrors we see. However, our spiritual evolution moves in leaps and bounds when we understand and embrace the mirrors.

Experiencing Oneness

At its highest level, divine oneness has only been experienced on earth by the few great masters—those who have been able to transcend the illusion of separation completely. There have been approximately 9000 ascended masters since the beginning of the experiment. There are also *living masters*—those who have achieved very high levels of spiritual evolution but are still in a body. These masters can move in and out of the state of oneness, but can only sustain that energy for a limited time.

Many of us have had brief experiences of the level of oneness that is required for our final Ascension in extraordinary moments of meditation. We can reach such a high state of bliss that it is easy to believe it cannot get any better. The yogis of the East warn their students not to be seduced by the incredible feeling of the high-level sutras they practice. They understand that the further we go, the more we know we have to learn. Both patience and humility are essential on our road to oneness.

In the next chapter, I use a model to demonstrate the many levels of evolution you must go through to reach oneness. It is attainable now. You simply need to understand the steps, accept where you are, and keep moving until you get there.

The State of Oneness

Divine oneness has seldom been achieved on this planet because it requires the total surrender of the physical, emotional, mental, and spiritual bodies. *Complete surrender* on all levels.

Oneness is a state of being. It is not something that can be done. It is a state of time that is endless, a state of space that does not exist. Oneness is unity with the visible and invisible at the same time. It is the undeniable end of the illusion of separation.

Once again, the English language is woefully inadequate for describing the experiences of the higher frequencies of spiritual evolution. The Eastern languages have words to identify these higher states of being, but even those descriptions can barely scratch the surface of the experience itself.

However, the dictionary defines oneness as a single unit with a single identity and a single mind, having freedom from discord and having unified thought, desire, and motive.[20] This definition is much the way I defined divine unity in the last chapter. As with unity, we need to create a new definition for spiritual evolution.

I define divine oneness as *the state of sensing and knowing no differences between any or all of the components of Source, completely unified in thought and feeling, and not only desiring but also knowing only the highest good of the whole.* While this sounds much like unity, it is a higher state only experienced after unity has been fully and completely mastered. It is a state of pure bliss beyond anything you can know in a human body and is your natural state in the 5th dimension.

---

[20] *Random House Webster's College Dictionary*, Random House, Inc., New York, NY, 1991.

In other words, it is the ability to fully and completely step out of the illusion of duality without one shred of the old lower-self remaining. It is complete healing of all the separation from Source in all ways. While many have come close to this state, few have mastered this final step out of the illusion. Again, as they teach in the East, the highest states of meditation before reaching oneness can be so enticing that you believe you have arrived. You can easily believe that it cannot get any better, but it can.

Cells in the Body of Source

One approach to understanding the structure of oneness is the analogy of human beings as "cells in the body of Source." This analogy is used by many teachers and is a perfect way to understand our connection to all creation.

The human body is made of trillions of cells. Each of those cells contains a strand of DNA that tells the cell everything about itself, its history, and the body of which it is a part. Coded into each cell—into the cellular memory—is the knowledge of this individual's past lifetimes, the plans and programs for this life, and the possibilities for the future. Coded into each cell are the cell's individual function, group function, and role in the whole body's health. This information is all in the DNA.

While each cell has its unique individual function, it also has a group function. Like cells come together in groups to create organs, glands, fibers, and tissues to perform group functions for the physical body's highest good. All of this is coded into the DNA such that each cell knows what it is to do.

Then, each of these different components—hair, skin, organs, glands, etc.—form systems. The systems—nervous, circulatory, digestive, etc.—organize and coordinate the group functions. This process is also programmed into the DNA of each cell. These systems come together to create an entire body—a living, breathing human being I will call "you."

Each of these cells is busy doing its job, focused on its little piece to create a happy, healthy you. You are not aware of the function of each tiny cell as long as you are feeling well. However, if a cell refuses to do its job or a group of cells moves out of alignment with your highest good, you no longer feel so well. When a group of cells is no longer working together for your highest good, disease and illness set in. If these cells are not healed, if these cells do not come back into alignment for your highest good, the symptoms worsen. If they recruit other cells to join them, your symptoms get much worse. If these cells do not shift back into alignment for your highest good, the disease created may eventually kill you. When the individual cells do not work together for your highest good, the entirety of who you are suffers and possibly dies. A healthy, happy you depends on each cell functioning in alignment with your highest good.

The process that applies to the cells of your body also applies to you as a cell in the body of Source. Coded into your DNA is your entire story—who you are as Source, what you are here to do, what you are here to heal for yourself, how you have come to serve, how you fit into the plan for human evolution, and more. You, as an individual cell, have a unique personal service. This service comes together with the unique services of others to create groups—the organs and glands. Those groups work together to create systems in the new paradigm designed to heal mass consciousness and create oneness for all humanity—a healed body.

When any cell in a human body is out of balance, out of alignment with the highest good, it creates dysfunction and puts the whole into stress. When any cell in the body of humanity is not working for the highest good of all, the whole suffers. The person on the other side of the world that you have never met is a cell in the body of humanity—your body! We are inseparable from any other member of the human race, and it is all in our DNA.

Human beings perceive themselves as very different from each other, yet most scientists today tell us that less than 3% of human DNA is different from person to person. Some scientists believe that we are as little as .3% different. Human evolution is the story of human beings moving apart from each other and, now, moving back together. While much of this truth has been shared through spiritual philosophy, science today is giving us more and more data to prove that the knowledge of the great mystics was correct—we are all one. We are all part of Source.

The Hologram

Another approach to the structure of oneness is to understand the hologram of creation. Simply put in metaphysical terms, a hologram is energy brought into form. In more scientific terms, a hologram is a multi-dimensional image created through the projection of light. In this case, your hologram is the projection of your light as Source.

In a hologram, many dynamics affect each aspect of the projection. A single particle from a hologram can be taken and used to create another identical hologram because in a hologram, what is known to the whole is known to the part, and what is known to the part is known to the whole. In other words, each part of a hologram knows (or is) the entire hologram.

You are an individual hologram. Each piece of your DNA knows everything about you. As your inner light shines through your DNA, a projection of your body and all that you are appears in physical form. As your inner light grows, the projection of your body becomes more light-filled. The truth of who you are as divine love must eventually shine throughout your hologram because that is who you are.

You are also part of the bigger hologram of the experiment. The experiment is part of the larger hologram of the universe, and so on. Everything is part of the hologram of Source. As each part of the hologram inside the experiment becomes more light-filled, the experiment heals. As the experiment heals, the hologram of Source evolves. We are part of All That Is.

The Interconnection of All Things

Moving into spiritual mastery is a choice. Moving into oneness with all things is a choice. The junk DNA and invisible strands of DNA, those we do not yet have the equipment to identify, connect us to all other human beings, Mother Earth, the Galactic Family, and beyond to all of creation, and All That Is. Unity and oneness are part of our structure. We are moving back into oneness as we are programmed to do.

As the frequencies of the planet and humanity move higher, our bodies begin to shift. As our DNA begins to resonate at higher frequencies, we begin to remember who we are. Because everyone in the body of humanity is connected through our DNA, when one person shifts, the entire body of humanity shifts, even if only a tiny bit. But, little by little, change happens in human mass consciousness until the point of critical mass is reached, and the shift back into oneness is unstoppable. Remember the hologram—what affects one of us affects all of us.

The body of humanity is shifting now. Our DNA is beginning to resonate with the higher frequencies of love and oneness. We are beginning to remember at the cellular level that we are one.

People at all levels of consciousness are feeling this shift. It is comfortable for a few, but uncomfortable for most because they do not realize what is happening in this change of consciousness. They do not understand why they feel so strange or why the old ways of being are falling apart. People feel edgy and out of sorts more than usual. They lose their tempers more easily and feel a stronger need to hold on to the old to maintain stability. When the lower-self fears losing what it believes to be true based on how things have always been, it wants to fight back. Aggressive reactions to the fear of loss and change are being seen worldwide.

At the same time, there is a growing sense of community and the need to work together to create change. As the sense of community grows, new ideas and solutions to the world's problems will arise, and more hope will be seen for the future. The masters have told us that we would come back into oneness, and it is happening now.

No More Secrets

Oneness means no more secrets because we are all part of the hologram, and separation is an illusion. Because you are part of Source, Source must be part of you. Because you are part of the whole, the whole must be part of you. It is how a hologram works. What Source knows, you must know, and what you know, Source must know.

If we allow ourselves to remember, we are each a master of the entire hologram. The exciting aspect of this knowledge is that we are each one with the mind of Source. There is nothing in the universe that we cannot know when we get our frequency high enough to surrender to that knowing. Imagine no more books or the internet—just ask and get clear answers.

The somewhat more frightening aspect of this for the lower-self is that there is no place to hide in oneness. Everyone knows everything.

"No more secrets" is two-fold. First, we can no longer hide from our truth when everyone has their psychic powers clearly activated. I always find it interesting when a student comes to me because of my abilities and then tries to cover up or hold back what is going on for them. We usually laugh when they realize what they are doing and that it does not work.

Second, and most importantly, we have nothing we want or need to hide when we have healed our fear, guilt, and shame. In the unconditional love of divine oneness, we are free of the judgments and fears that drive us to the secrecy we seek inside the illusion. Oneness gives us the complete freedom to be ourselves, knowing that we are always loved, no matter what. It allows us to grow, learn, and expand as our true creator selves, free of restraints and ego-desires.

Choosing Oneness

Oneness cannot be done; it must be experienced. Someone can tell you about oneness or give you exercises or practices to follow to bring you into a state of oneness, but no one can do oneness for you. Oneness comes through a shift of consciousness. It comes through a series of experiences that change who you are. Oneness is achieved on your own. We each have a great deal of support in both the physical and spiritual realms, but it is only through individual effort that you achieve the experience.

Oneness happens as you master your light. The light must grow and radiate from within. Light can be brought in from the outside as part of the healing process and to help you remember who you are. However, as you break through your darkness, you understand that the light of Source shines from within. The light outside you is not your source. Only the light inside you is your source. Your guides, teachers, and angels are not your source. The Christ is not your source. Your inner light is your source. Therefore, you must master your light to move back into oneness.

Only when you have attained the state of oneness that you knew before the experiment can you graduate to your final Ascension from Earth and move into the next phase of your evolution, wherever that may be. You cannot skip the steps. You can make them easier or harder, take them faster or slower, but you cannot skip them. Everyone goes through the same stages of spiritual expansion to achieve oneness.

Oneness is achieved by choice. It is the complete surrender of the physical, emotional, mental, and spiritual aspects of who you are to a state of total connection with the divine and no remaining separation. Only at that level of surrender to the whole are you ready for Ascension with a capital *A*. Change and surrender are not high on the to-do list for most people, yet these are required for ending the Experiment in Duality.

Achieving Oneness Through Mirrors

I was introduced to the principle of mirrors in 1997 through the Seven Essene Mirrors described by Gregg Braden in his book *Walking between the Worlds: The Science of Compassion.*[21] The Essenes were an ancient mystery school, many of whom we know as ascended masters, including Master Jesus and his father, Joseph.

The Essenes taught mirrors in seven basic categories, in which all mirrors could be found. Again, the principle is that we cannot see something in another person (or in a situation) unless it is also a part of us; therefore, everyone we see is a reflection of who we are at any point in time. Whether someone impresses you or pushes your buttons, it reflects you.

When I first read the principle of mirrors, it made perfect sense to me. I continued to encounter the teaching of mirrors in almost everything I read in my spiritual studies. However, I did not truly refine my understanding and use of mirrors in my process until I began to study with Kris. As I mastered the reflections of myself in the world, my judgments diminished, and my spiritual growth accelerated. Mirrors have become a significant part of my evolution. I especially enjoy the shift from having my buttons pushed

[21] Braden, Greg, *Walking between the Worlds: the Science of Compassion*, Radio Bookstore Press, 1997.

to experiencing ease, joy, and beauty as my frequency continues to go higher.

Everyone is a mirror of who we are because, beneath the illusion, we are all one. In a way, we have volunteered to assist each other on this journey by reflecting to each other how far we have come *and* how far we still have to go. What a wonderful tool to use. What a fantastic tool to push us out of denial of ourselves as creators.

Mirrors are simple, but they can be elusive because they can be subtle and often reflect the issues we would rather not accept as our own. The Standing in the Light® program dedicates quite a bit of time to "walls, buttons, and mirrors" because these are the ways our souls and the universe show us who we are. There are many ways to approach the subject of mirrors.

If you are drawn to the Seven Essene Mirrors, I recommend going to an original version from the Essene Mystery School instead of one of the contemporary versions. The modern versions are very good, but the original takes you into more depth. If you follow the Eastern traditions, consider the yoga sutra of Patanjali that says, "Then the Seer (Self) abides in Its own nature."[22]

Oneness of the Male and Female

Another significant and possibly the ultimate challenge in the journey back into oneness is healing and merging the male and female within. As with everything else, your inner male and female must be in harmony, cooperation, unity, and oneness. The male and female energies have been separated within humanity for a very long time due to the experiment. However, they must come back together in oneness to end duality and prepare for Ascension.

Source is both male and female. We call the male and female creative components of Source the God/Goddess. All paths that lead to Ascension teach the importance of both the divine male and divine female within. This

---

[22] Satchidananda, Swami. *The Yoga Sutras of Patanjali: Commentary on the Raja Yoga Sutras by Sri Swami Satchidananda* (p. 23). Integral Yoga Publications. Kindle Edition.

energy has nothing to do with gender. It is about the masculine and feminine qualities that create a whole, what is often referred to as the Mother/Father God.

The Hindus and Buddhists have always taught the importance of the male and the female. Even Christianity has its roots in the divine female as much as the divine male, though those teachings became well hidden under Constantine.

For example, Genesis 1:26-27 describes "God's" decision to create humanity.

> Then God said, 'Let *us* make humankind in *our* image, according to *our* likeness; and let them have dominion over the fish of the sea, and over the birds of the air, and over the cattle, and over all the wild animals of the earth, and over every creeping thing that creeps upon the earth.' So God created humankind in his image, *in the image of God he created them; male and female he created them.*[23]

The Apocrypha is a group of chapters from the original version of *The Bible* that speak of Sophia, the female wisdom and creative energy of God. While these chapters are still included in the Catholic bible, they have been removed from most protestant versions. The early Christian tradition was steeped in the worship of the female as well as the male aspects of God. Women were often ordained and taught the gospel.

The God/Goddess are not beings outside ourselves but are aspects of Source essential to creative energy. Like us, they exist inside Source as offices in the Spiritual Hierarchy and are one with All That Is. Neither is superior nor inferior to the other. They are just different frequencies of Source serving different and essential functions in the universe.

The male and female forces are always present in creation, whether they are recognized or not. This union is often challenging to understand because of the lower-self's version of what male and female mean. The male

---

[23] Genesis 1:26-27, *NRSV Bible with the Apocrypha*, Kindle Edition, HarperCollins, New York, NY, 2011.

and female qualities perceived by gender and societal traditions are not the complete picture and not the proper male and female balance of the divine male and female.

The female is the seed with which everything begins. Whether it is a physical seed that grows into a living thing or the seed of an idea that blossoms into some form of creation, the initial intention from which anything comes into form is female energy. The female receives and nurtures the idea. The female energy is the being state—the still and quiet space from which ideas are born.

The male energy is the action state—the movement of energy into the idea or intention to bring it into form. The male is the doer. His role is to get things done.

Creation requires both concept and action. Without her seed, there is nothing to create. Without his action, nothing gets done, and nothing comes into form.

The divine male and female have nothing to do with gender as we perceive it in human form. The divine understands that everything in the universe must have both male and female energy to survive and that the power must be in balance to maintain harmony. When your male and female are out of balance, you have problems. The energy either runs wild without direction or thought as to the highest good or sits inert until everything crumbles. Either way, imbalance means chaos and destruction. Alone, neither he nor she can work well. Together, they work brilliantly.

The male and female energies always work together to create. She creates the idea and holds the intention. He moves the energy into the intention to bring the idea into form. Because one does not happen without the other, you can see that the male and female energies have always been present in each of us. Everything you have ever created has had both male and female components, or you could not have created it.

The challenge for the lower-self is understanding the two, embracing them, and bringing them back into perfect balance. To do this, you must put gender traits aside and focus on the divine male and female characteristics within us all. What became separated due to the Experiment in Duality must be brought back together and merged into oneness. Both need to be honored, and both need to be trusted. Have I said yet that what is simple is not always easy?

Oneness as Sovereign Creators

If you are created from Source, you must be part of Source. If you are part of Source, you must be part of the hologram. If you are part of the hologram, you must be operating with others, whether you realize it or not. What you choose to create inside the hologram affects the entire hologram.

You are the center of your universe, but your universe exists inside the body of Source. You have the ability and the right to create everything your soul desires for you. However, while we are each the creators of our reality, we are also co-creators with all other things, which means that everything we create affects everything else in creation, every aspect of the hologram. Each creation affects and impacts others. The balance of creatorship with co-creatorship is essential to coming back into oneness.

The Law of Attraction says that like energy attracts like energy. This law tells you that you can only create circumstances that align with the energies you hold, even though those energies may be subconscious and seemingly unknown to you. Under the Law of Attraction, you must create it all. No one and no thing can be a victim, even though it is easy to feel that way.

This principle is how we help each other learn and grow, whether our community is our family or the whole planet. We act and react. These actions mirror our lessons to each other so that we can identify and heal what is keeping us from the experience of oneness.

You do, however, have the choice to create consciously or unconsciously. Creating at the level of oneness is choosing to create for the highest good of all, checking with your guidance, and following the higher frequency plan.

You cannot achieve oneness and the experience of yourself as Source in isolation. You cannot do it alone. You must do it *as* one if you are to *be* one. Yet, you must know that you are the creator of your journey with all the Power of Source. If you accept that you are creating your journey and your experiences, you must accept that everyone else is creating theirs.

Remembering Who We Are

What I have described is not just New Age babble. What I learned in the New Age teachings from the Christ is also reflected in the ancient teachings, as in this passage from Sri Swami Satchidananda in *The Yoga Sutras of Patanjali.*

> You seem to have lost your original identity and have identified with your thoughts and your body. Suppose I ask you who you are. If you say, "I am a man," you have identified yourself with a masculine body. If you say, "I am a professor," you are identifying with the ideas gathered in your brain. If you say, "I am a millionaire," you are identifying with your bank account; if "a mother," with a child; "a husband," with a wife. "I am tall; I am short; I am black or white" shows your identity with the shape and color of your body. But without any identifications, who are you? Have you ever thought about it? When you really understand that, you will see we are all the same. If you detach yourself completely from all the things you have identified yourself with, you realize yourself as pure "I." In that pure "I" there is no difference between you and me.
>
> This is true not only with human beings, but with everything. You call something a dog because it has a dog's body. The spirit in a dog and a human is the same. The same is true even with inanimate objects; there is the same spirit in a stone or a wall. If I use the term "spirit," or "Self," you might hesitate to believe me, but if a physicist says the wall is nothing but energy, you will believe that. So, using the scientist's language, there is nothing but energy everywhere. Even the atom is a form of energy. The same energy appears in different forms to which we also give names. So the form and the name are just different versions of the same energy. And, according to the Yoga

> scientists, such as Patanjali—and even many modern scientists—behind the different forms of energy is one unchanging consciousness or spirit or Self.[24]

You are on a journey of remembering who you are as Source. You are moving from the perception that you are limited and separate to the knowing that you are unlimited and one. When you identify with your human emotions, you are identifying with your lower-self. When you identify with the feeling states of your soul, you identify with your self-as-Source. When you identify only with those feeling states of your self-as-Source, you will know true oneness and your full power.

The Growth of All Creation through Oneness

All of creation exists inside the body of Source. Because what is known to the part is also known to the whole, Source learns and grows through your experiences. You are not an empty vessel allowing divine energy to work through you. You *are* the energy. You are an expression of Source and all the power and the wisdom that comes from knowing yourself as One.

Source is ever-expanding. Source does not grow through observing us. Source experiences and feels what we experience and feel because we are part of Source. We are one unit—one creation existing at different levels of consciousness and different levels of learning. Like a school system with first and second graders, up to twelfth graders, everyone has a place, and everyone moves up the educational scale one grade at a time. However, Source is never-ending, which means our education is never-ending. We graduate from one level to the next through eternity. We are ever-growing and ever-expanding.

Just as the cells of our bodies are one within us, all things are one within the body of Source. One may ask why we are not aware of All That Is happening for every cell in our bodies the way Source is aware of what is

---

[24] Sri Swami Satchidananda, *The Yoga Sutras of Patanjali: Commentary on the Raja Yoga Sutras by Sri Swami Satchidananda*, Integral Yoga® Publications, Buckingham, VA, 2012, 7.

happening in every cell of its body. Most of humanity is simply not yet at the level of consciousness to believe it can.

If we look at the stories of the Eastern masters in books like *The Life and Teachings of the Masters of the Far East*[25] and *The Autobiography of a Yogi*[26], we find examples of those who have learned to connect to, trust, and utilize the mind of Source—full living masters. We are all capable of this same level of awareness and the creation of miracles. However, to do so, we must get our frequencies high enough, and our "little minds" quiet.

Participation in the experiment decreased our frequency such that we could no longer access our connection to the mind of Source—the one mind. Our journey back into oneness, and into Ascension, is the process of healing what blocks that connection. Everything in creation is a unique expression of Source, but there is ultimately only one consciousness for All That Is.

---

[25] Spalding, Baird, *The Life and Teachings of the Masters of the Far East*, Devross & Co., Camarillo, CA, 1986.

[26] Paramahansa Yogananda , *Autobiography of a Yogi*, 13th edition, The International Publications of Self-Realization Fellowship, Los Angeles, CA, 1998.

Chapter 8

The Levels of Avatar

He who tastes a grain of mustard seed knows more of its flavor than he who sees an elephant load of it.
—Hindu Proverb

The level of consciousness of those we call living masters can feel unattainable. Most of humanity will not achieve that level of mastery in this life. However, many will, and many more will get very close. It is not a hop, skip, and jump from our first awakening to oneness.

The further we go, the more we know we have to learn. We move through multiple stages of evolution on our journey from newly awakened lightworkers to masters. The masters who have gone before us have tried to explain these stages in different ways, giving us various models. These models have been designed to help us understand the process we are moving through and provide the lower-self something to hold on to as we venture into unknown territory.

The Nature of Personal Frequencies is a model shared in Standing in the Light® that traces the scale of human evolution from the densest emotional experiences to the experience of oneness. I share another model in the next chapter. The Nature of Personal Frequencies condenses the hundreds of emotional experiences into a scale of seventy-two to make it manageable. It begins at the bottom with hatred and anger and moves up the octaves of human emotions to trust and compassion.

When you have moved to the top of the scale of human emotions, you begin to shift into the "feeling states" of spiritual mastery. When you start this shift, you move into the upper levels of personal frequencies called the Nine Levels of Avatar.

The Nature of Personal Frequencies

The Nature of Personal Frequencies is a channeled model that has been passed down for decades.[27] Understanding the shift from the "human" frequencies to "master" frequencies is key to understanding the difference in emotions and feeling states.

The terms *emotions* and *feelings* are two more words that are often used interchangeably in the 3rd dimension but serve us better in the 4th-dimensional transition if we define them differently.

- *Emotions* are knee-jerk reactions to the outer world. If something happens that we have defined as good, we have a positive emotional response. If something happens that we have defined as bad, we have a negative emotional response. The key components are judgment, belief, the outer world, and knee-jerk (no control).

- *Feelings* are the inner states of being that are becoming a part of who we are, no matter what is happening in the outer world. We cannot transcend the illusion if we rely on or allow what is happening around us or to us to determine how we feel and respond. For example, we must feel love and joy, no matter what happens in the outer world. Spiritual mastery exists above the scale of human emotions.

---

[27] The original source of The Nature of Personal Frequencies has retired from public life and has asked not to be acknowledged as of this printing. He has been gracious in allowing his material to be shared in this book.

Let's say a woman believes that a man brings flowers because he loves her and likes giving her little surprises. When her guy walks in the door with a bouquet of her favorite flowers, she lights up and gives him a hug and kiss. All is well.

On the opposite side, let's say a woman believes a man brings flowers because he has done something wrong and is trying to soften the bad news. The response is entirely different when her guy walks in the door with a bouquet of her favorite flowers. She bristles, puts her hands on her hips, and asks what he's done wrong. No hugs and kisses here, even if his intentions are loving.

Both of these are emotional responses. They are both knee-jerk reactions to something that happened in the outer world. One is more loving, and one is less loving, but both are emotional responses.

In the spiritual world of feeling states, the state of love is who we are at all times, no matter what happens outside ourselves. The state of joy is who we are at all times, no matter what happens outside us. We can still enjoy the surprise of a loving bouquet. A box of chocolates might be even better for some. However, nothing outside of ourselves is needed to make us feel good, and nothing outside of ourselves can take us out of our divine state.

Using these definitions, we can understand that trust and compassion, for example, exist both as emotions and as feeling states. The emotions of trust and compassion are lower frequencies than the feeling states of divine trust and compassion. All that we consider positive emotions must be mastered at the basic human level and then mastered on the spiritual level of an avatar.

The Nature of Personal Frequencies is another version of climbing the spiral staircase. The details of the system are not important. However, the concept is essential because spiritual students must understand that we all have many steps to climb before entering the world of those we know as masters. We can all get there, but only one step at a time. We cannot skip steps, but we can choose to walk or run up the staircase. Whether walking or running up the staircase, we keep going.

As you read the following, remember that we are each a master in the making. We each have issues to rise above, but we are always moving toward our ultimate mastery. No matter where we might be on the scale of The Nature of Personal Frequencies, we are all moving up the spiral staircase to the time when we "get it" and step into the realm of an avatar.

You will crisscross the various levels of any system because there are no clear-cut lines between the stages of evolution. You will often have one foot on one level and another foot on another. Sometimes it will feel like you have run out of feet because you are taking two or three steps forward in one area but are stuck in others. Just keep walking.

The Nine Avatar Frequencies

Many believe that someone must be born an avatar to experience those frequencies in a given lifetime. They do not believe someone can move from a lower level in the conga line to that of an avatar in a single life. Fortunately, the experiences of many masters show us differently.

I define an avatar as a spiritual master, not just a great teacher. Many can "master" and share the teachings, but an avatar also models through walking the talk, such as Masters Jesus, Yogananda, Amma, Kwan Yin, and others. In the following model, we move through nine levels of an avatar to reach oneness.

I am only giving an overview of the Nine Levels of Avatar here. Within each of the nine are many sub-levels of mastery. We begin the journey into avatar when we embrace ourselves not only as spiritual beings but also as part of Source. This first level is called Enlightenment.

Enlightenment

The word enlightenment is defined differently in different spiritual practices. In this model, Enlightenment is *the moment when one awakens to the understanding that Source is inside and outside of us at the same time.* This energy refers to the concept that Source is not a being outside us, creating and controlling us; instead, we are part of Source. If we are cells in the body of Source, the God/Goddess must be both within and around us at the same time.

It is one thing to say Source is everywhere and that we are all part of Source. It is another to actually *get it.* Enlightenment is the awakening to the full understanding we are Source. However, at the first level of avatar, this understanding is still a concept and not yet one's reality.

Enlightenment is a big step. Once we understand this concept, everything starts to change. The idea that "we are all one" takes on new meaning and new experiences. The energy of Enlightenment was seeded on a large scale in the 1960s and 70s with the hippies and the flower children. The standard of "make love, not war" was the influence of the energy of Enlightenment. However, the planet's overall energy was too dense for the power of Enlightenment to maintain a stronghold. While it faded into the background, it has never been lost and is currently being resurrected on the planet. The level of Enlightenment will be achieved by many in this lifetime. It will continue to grow in the generations to come until all humanity knows that we are one with Source.

Euphoria

Euphoria is *the experience of effortless flow and the awareness that one is coming into a greater sense of the love of all things.* In Euphoria, we recognize that we are shifting into awareness more than thought. We are learning more from our insights than from teachings. We just seem to know and understand things we did not know or understand before. These experiences may only be momentary at first, but they grow in number and consistency.

In Euphoria, we also experience more moments of "being in the flow" or being "in the zone." We have all experienced those moments when nothing can go wrong, and everything is effortless. Imagine living in that state at all times. We are designed to be effortless flow in creation.

Self-Realization

Self-Realization is *the point when Enlightenment is not just a concept but an experience.* We are now beginning to experience ourselves as perfection. The expression of unconditional love and the desire to surrender to Divine Will grows. We find that our lives have more balance, especially the balance of giving and receiving. Abundance in all forms is beginning to flow more effortlessly.

Self-Realization is the beginning of the actual experience of ourselves as Source. It is one thing to understand this principle intellectually, and it is another to incorporate it into our being such that it is the *experience* of life. Self-Realization is the beginning of the experience of true oneness. While someone may feel they have reached this level and may have, Self-Realization is a very high frequency. Great masters, such as Sai Baba, Yogananda, and Jesus, were born at this level of consciousness.

Transcendence

Lacking words to describe this experience, Spirit defines Transcendence as simply *more Self-Realized.* In Transcendence, we are moving further into the desire for Divine Will and the highest good of all. The sense of *me* and the lower-self as separate from Source is merging into the sense of *we* and oneness with All That Is.

This stage of the avatar range is subtle. During this phase, our knowingness of ourselves as Source is amplified. We are gaining more identity as part of Source in preparation for the next stage of growth.

Expansion

Expansion is *when the divine energy moving through the body begins to expand on the atomic level.* Now we are bringing more light into the body. Our frequency is going much higher, and the atoms of our bodies need to expand.

Consider spinning a pendulum, or a bobble, on a string. If the bobble is spinning at a slow speed (what I will call low frequency), the bobble makes small, gentle circles. It does not pull tightly against the string. However, if the speed increases (what I will call higher frequency), the size of the circle increases, and the bobble pulls against the string in an effort to expand the circle's size.

This expansion is happening inside the human body as our frequency goes higher. The energy at the atomic level of our bodies is moving faster, and the atoms in our bodies feel as though they are getting bigger and trying to grow beyond our bodies. In some ways, they are, which creates very strange sensations and, sometimes, fear for the lower-self unless one understands what is happening.

However, there is a principle of the physics of infinity that reminds us that something can not only grow infinitely larger, but it can also grow infinitely smaller. The divine energy moving through us and expanding on the atomic level is designed to expand infinitely inside of us. We will not explode, even though it sometimes feels that way.

Soul Mate Reunion

Soul Mate Reunion is *the awareness of moving into divine unity with the totality of one's soul and all of one's being.* At Soul Mate Reunion, all aspects of Self merge into a higher state of oneness. We begin to feel the completeness of who we are at all levels as we merge into oneness with all aspects of our soul (our Soul Mates). We realize that we see almost everything from our soul's perspective with love, compassion, and non-judgment.

This experience is not the soul mate of human myth. We have no one perfect person designed to make us whole. We *are* whole. The desire to find the perfect counterpart is the desire to merge our inner male and female back into unity. It does not mean we cannot have partners and enjoy that aspect of human life. It does mean that we need no one outside of ourselves to make us feel whole or complete. Remember who you are.

Pure Joy

Pure Joy is *the experience of ecstatic divine love while in the body.* At Pure Joy, we have the total awareness of being one with the divine, yet we still feel the separation of having a physical body. Pure Joy has rarely been felt on earth until now. In the past, most masters felt so wonderful in this experience that they did not realize they had not reached complete oneness. Now, with an awareness of where we are in our evolution and a process for moving into the state of oneness, more and more of us will be able to attain this ultimate state of unity that moves us on to Ascension.

Self-Activation

Self-Activation is *the transition, or the doorway, through which one must pass to get from Pure Joy to divine oneness.* In this model, all stages of avatar up to this point can be achieved through meditation and energy techniques that raise our frequency. However, oneness is a choice and must be self-initiated. Our souls will not take away our power by doing it for us. We must want it with all we are and make it our choice.

Oneness

Oneness is *the ultimate experience of divine unity with All That Is.* Oneness is fully coming home, like a drop of rainwater merging back into the ocean. It is the final step before Ascension. We still have a body at this level of mastery, but we are moving in and out of light.

In Oneness, the heart stops beating, breathing ceases, and all lower bodies surrender to a momentary death. All of our dominant frequencies must be in the avatar range to enter the state of divine oneness. None of the lower frequency human emotions can be present to experience this level of ourselves as one with Source.

The Importance of Meditation

Meditation comes first, last, and always on the road to oneness. Oneness is a state of being, not doing. The ability to get out of the lower bodies, especially the mental body, is essential. Remember, oneness is the *total* surrender of the lower-self. The physical world is an illusion. We cannot remember and experience ourselves-as-Source while attached to the illusion. The silence of meditation and the reconnection that occurs in a deep meditative state are what we need to remember who we are.

The Road to Mastery

Moving from the consciousness of the lower-self to the higher-self is simply a matter of climbing up the staircase. It may take a long time or a short time, but we all end up at mastery. It is who we are.

All aspects of who you are do not move up the scale at the same rate. Some issues will be mastered before others depending on what you have packed in your spiritual suitcase. It is not only possible, but it is also the norm for people to hold a wide range of frequencies at any point in time. You can be at an avatar level on one issue and down deep into the emotional levels on another.

The point is to understand where you are going and just keep moving until everything is healed. Sing, dance, laugh, and enjoy even the bumps in the road. It is your creation. Committing to your mastery is a big deal. Mastery requires dedication and discipline in daily practice and allowing change. The masters who have gone before us made the choices to follow their chosen paths. We simply need to do the same.

Chapter 9

The Levels of Initiation

Do not be conformed to this world, but be transformed
by the renewing of your minds, so that you may
discern what is the will of God.
—Romans 12:2, *The NRSV Bible*

There is no one right way to reach Ascension. There is no right or wrong way to do it and no right or wrong way to track or evaluate one's progress. However, over the centuries of spiritual evolution, great teachers have provided various methods to help us know where we are on our road home.

Another method to help us understand spiritual evolution and know where we might be on the road is called levels of initiation. Again, these are just models designed to guide students on their way to oneness, and there are many. If you do a computer search on spiritual levels of initiation, you will find numerous versions—Hindu, Buddhist, New Age, Theosophy, Gnostic, Sufi, Egyptian, Starseed, and more.

I have studied many programs about levels of initiation and found five to twenty-four levels of light in the different systems. Each system has similar yet varied definitions of what each level means. If you were to compare this to other systems, you would find many similarities and learn they all will work. The one that works best for me through my studies is still the one I learned from Kris. It has served me well in understanding what it means to become a living master and ascend.

In general, an initiation is a ceremony allowing a rite of passage, whether moving into adulthood, joining an organization, or achieving an honor. Under this definition, an initiation is a ritual performed by one person for another for a specific purpose. It is an acknowledgment and usually follows a specific format.

In the spiritual world, an initiation is the attainment of a specific amount, or level, of light. As your frequency goes higher, the amount of light in your body (your light quotient) increases. The more light you hold in your body, the higher your level of consciousness and the closer to oneness you become.

The Six Levels of Initiation described below take many lifetimes to achieve. However, based on the higher frequencies of the planet and the higher frequency energy techniques available now, the process can move more quickly. The levels of initiation help you understand how the scale of human frequency forms the conga line and how the conga line is moving forward one light quotient at a time. They also explain human behavior at different levels of light and, hopefully, allow you to release judgment of yourself (and others) for where you are in your process. Whether you ever employ this information directly or not, understanding this process is helpful.

A human being can only understand life and only perform in life according to the amount of light they hold at any point in time. Only when our frequency goes higher can we shift to higher consciousness and enable lasting change. Only when we increase our light can we move from the first grade to the second to the third, and so on. It has always been about our light.

As we approach the study of any system of initiation, we are well served to remain in humility. As so many masters have pointed out to their students so many times, where we want to be, where we think we are, and where we actually are, are not necessarily the same. Honesty with ourselves is critical to our wisdom and our progress.

The Six Levels of Initiation

Entire books are written about the various levels of initiation from around the planet. This model of levels of initiation contains six levels of light, or six initiations. Each has many sub-levels that I will not try to share here. Likewise, I would need another book to explain the many steps and subtleties of moving through each initiation, why they are important, and why we cannot skip steps.

I have included information on the levels of initiation as an insight into the spiritual process and the time, compassion, and patience needed to go from a fledgling lightworker to a living master. I am giving a brief overview of each level, including:

- the light quotient
- the definition, the motivations, and the goals
- the general characteristics and actions
- the dominant energies

These descriptions provide a taste of what is to come, no matter where you may be on their journey at the moment. The levels of initiation are important to an overall understanding of the experiment and the stages each of us must go through to graduate.

Pre-Awakening

There are two stages of consciousness that human beings must move through before reaching the First Level of Initiation—the first level of spiritual consciousness. The first of those is Pre-Awakening. A relatively large percentage of the human population is still at this stage. These are the blessed ones at the end of the conga line, chugging along as the conga line moves forward. In Pre-Awakening, one does not believe in any form of god or creator and does not care. This group is only activated to the second chakra and is focused on day-to-day survival and enjoyment. They do not care about how they got here, the purpose of human existence, or even the most primary spiritual needs.

At some point in time, every one of us was in Pre-Awakening. As the conga line entered the experiment, we each entered this phase of lower consciousness as part of our agreement to forget who we were as light and learn about the little will of man. As the head of the conga line moved higher in frequency and out of Pre-Awakening, the end of the conga line moved into Pre-Awakening. Nothing is *wrong* with those who are still at this stage. They simply got there later than others because they volunteered to anchor the back of the line. They will get their turn at the next stage as the line moves forward.

Pre-Awakening is not the same as atheism. Those in Pre-Awakening simply give little or no thought to a God or any creative force in the universe. Those who identify themselves as atheists have considered these matters and have decided there is no God. Much of this goes to how God is defined, which is tricky, as I discussed in the introduction. Each person has the divine right to choose their beliefs.

First Awakening

The First Awakening is the next stage before entering the First Level of Initiation. Those at First Awakening are aware that there must be something *out there* that created everything, but they have no firm beliefs about who or what God is to them. They may try to follow a religion, but the meaning of the teachings and traditions elude them. Their primary goal is to belong to something. Their views will most likely be quite dogmatic, and they will have a strong need to protect and defend what they think they believe.

These are good people. Like those at Pre-Awakening, they are holding their place in the conga line and moving one step at a time into more light. Because their level of light is still low, they are easily led by charismatic figures and look to those outside themselves to tell them what is right or wrong. They are led more by fear than other motivators. This group also makes up a large part of the current population.

Those at the First Awakening encompass members of all religions, New Age, and even atheists. Those at this level are trying to find something to believe and someone to help them figure it out. Without the set of beliefs established during the First Awakening, one does not have a foundation for moving into the First Level of Initiation. This stage of evolution is critical.

The First Level of Initiation

The First Level of Initiation begins when one holds 5% light. At this level, one believes in a god (a creator), and believers are very sure of their beliefs. They believe God is outside of us (separate from us), strict, and judgmental, but "He" is also becoming very personal. God now has a meaning for believers that did not exist at lower levels of light.

At the First Level of Initiation, one begins to truly want to feel their connection to Source, what they believe to be God. This step is huge. Spiritual beliefs are no longer superficial. These people want to be good examples of what they believe is right.

People at this level are primarily fear-driven because they believe in a judgmental and punishing God. They feel the need to confess their sins, to keep each other on the straight and narrow, and to do penance. They have a strong need to spread the word, to give testimony—give witness. The first level initiate blames the lower-self, or the ego-self, for everything wrong. The ego is bad and needs to be eliminated. The ego is their block to being one with God.

Those at the first level still need an outside leader; only now, this leader may be without a body. Jesus, Buddha, and Krishna are examples of those who might take a dominant role over another human being, such as a priest. The leader still needs to tell them what to do, and receiving blessings from the leader is very important.

The dominant energies at this level are fear and judgment. However, there is also the beginning of an opening of the heart. People are truly seeking the experience of peace, joy, love, and heaven on earth. They just believe in a strict and painful road to get there.

The Second Level of Initiation

The Second Level of Initiation begins when one holds 20% light. One still believes God is outside us at this level, but now God is loving and forgiving. Redemption comes through love and forgiveness, not through punishment.

At the Second Level of Initiation, one genuinely desires to understand the great truths and not just be told what to do. The desire to understand creates the desire to connect directly to the great teachers, both spiritual and philosophical. They want spiritual evolution. They want to do what is right for all of humanity and bring about positive change for the world.

People at this level study a wide variety of material from religious teachings to great philosophers. They want to figure out what they believe and why. They may learn to meditate and spend much time in contemplation or prayer. They begin to focus on inner healing, not just controlling their behavior. They are looking for lasting change. They are also likely to join organizations that work toward resolving social issues and world challenges.

Those at this level still seek outside leadership, but look to what they consider the great minds and leaders in their field. In New Age, this sometimes means channeled information. However, at the Second Level of Initiation, people usually look to others to channel information for them and do not yet consider their guidance to be a high enough source.

Everyone at this level seeks to expand themselves, no matter their chosen religious or spiritual path. The dominant energies here are more broadly loving in that there is a desire to help heal the world, regardless of the usual prejudices. People are moving into greater wisdom as well as greater peace, joy, and love.

The Third Level of Initiation

The Third Level of Initiation begins when one holds 36% light and represents a significant change for the initiate. In 2009, less than 3% of the human population reached the Third Level of Initiation. This number is significant. The third level has not been easily achieved and takes dedication to daily practice for completion. Just because one has been studying and gaining knowledge from those studies does not necessarily mean one is holding enough light to have integrated the energy and achieved this level of initiation. In 2020, the percentage of humanity that has reached the third level was slightly higher. We are making steady progress.

At the Third Level of Initiation, one truly understands that God, or Source, is within. This understanding is still intellectual and equates to the level of Enlightenment in the Nine Levels of Avatar in the last chapter. At this level, one is shifting dramatically from outer world focus to inner world focus. The lower-self is consciously beginning to connect directly to Source and to feel that the physical world is an illusion. Finding one's life purpose and spiritual service becomes a prime motivation.

People at this level are no longer looking for leaders outside of themselves. They are now looking for teachers. They understand that true wisdom and knowledge is within because God is within, and they look for those who can help them learn to access their inner wisdom.

The dominant energies are becoming more feminine. The expansion of light at the Third Level of Initiation creates a shift from seeing the creator as male to seeing the creator as both male and female. In other words, God is becoming the God/Goddess. This change initiates the need to feel the balance of the divine masculine and the divine feminine energies.

Completing the Third Level of Initiation takes as much energy and dedication as the First and Second Levels combined. The average lightworker in 2009 held 39-44% light. Many will not move beyond the Third Level of Initiation in this lifetime. But the third level is a huge accomplishment, and more of humanity is likely to achieve it this time around.

I could give percentages for 2020 and beyond, but I would prefer that everyone learn to channel clearly and get that information for themselves. Moreover, these numbers are just window dressing. They mean very little except to show us where we might be individually on our journey and where humanity might be as a whole. If the numbers are used to compare ourselves to others, judgment and competition have taken over. These percentages demonstrate the movement of the conga line and (hopefully) keep us in humility.

The Fourth Level of Initiation

The Fourth Level of Initiation begins when one holds 58% light. These are the highest levels of mastery on the planet. Less than .02% of humanity has ever achieved levels four and five combined.

The Fourth Level of Initiation is the complete renunciation of the physical world. The only motivation is the desire to experience oneness with All That Is and move entirely beyond the limits of the illusion. At this level, the outer world no longer holds any importance. Masters at this level are looking for inner success and no longer desire outer success. Spiritual evolution and dedication to service are all that matter.

Renunciation of the physical world does *not* mean poverty. It means the complete understanding and mastery of the physical illusion. One no longer gives power to the outer world. One knows spiritual truth and can purely be in this world, but not of it.

Master Jesus was born into the Fourth Level of Initiation. Ancient manuscripts found in the archives of European churches describe his childhood miracles and uncanny wisdom. While many people do not believe in miracles, I have seen too many unexplained phenomena not to believe in the stories of the loaves and fishes and other miracles performed by the Christ and other great masters.

When Jesus reportedly died on the cross, he was making his transition from the Fourth to the Fifth Level of Initiation. What appeared to be dying and rising again from the dead was his demonstration that the physical world is not real, that the body is not real, and that anything physical can be overcome. Granted, he chose what most would say was a very painful way to do this, but the example was remarkable. And do we know that it was painful? Had he transcended the physical world such that his experience was different from what you or I could perceive? I believe so.

The teachings of Jesus as the Christ never mentioned pain and suffering as a way home. Remember that the concept that he died for our sins was not part of the original doctrine. It was invented under Constantine. I believe that Jesus was a true master who knew no victimization. Instead, he created a remarkable scenario to gain the world's attention to show us what human beings can become.

The dominant energies of a master at level four are divine self-esteem, perfection, fulfillment, and divinity. The strength and experience of one's self-as-Source are too strong to be denied.

The Fifth Level of Initiation

The Fifth Level of Initiation begins when one holds 62% light. It is the final level of initiation before Ascension and the position of a living master. We are all masters in that all the answers lie inside us, and we have the power to access and live as Source. However, until the highest frequencies of consciousness are realized, we are merely masters in training.

The title of "Master" is often used for teachers at the Second, Third, and Fourth Levels of Initiation. Indeed, many have mastered teachings and skills at the various stages of evolution and are to be honored. However, we will all be better served by defining for ourselves what mastery is and why we call anyone a master. To the Spiritual Hierarchy, only the fifth-level initiates are true masters.

The fifth level was the final level before Ascension because, until now, the human body could not hold more than 73% light and remain in form. The Hindu master Paramahansa Yogananda is a perfect example of having reached his ultimate growth in a physical form and choosing to surrender his body.

Those who were present with Yogananda the last weeks and the last day of his life say that he had been planting the seed that he would soon be leaving. On March 7, 1952, he gave a speech at a dinner in Los Angeles. He concluded with a reading from the poem *My India*: "Where Ganges, woods, Himalayan caves, and men dream God—I am hallowed; my body touched that sod." At that time, his body fell, and he was gone.

While some people will dispute this, what Yogananda demonstrated was traditional Ascension. It is the way most of those ready to ascend in this life will make the transition—a simple surrender of the human form.[28] We have a small handful of living masters on the planet today who have expanded to 77-78% light, but they are still far from the new lightbody that is the Sixth Level of Initiation.

The Sixth Level of Initiation

The Sixth Level of Initiation begins at 74% light. It has never been achieved in a human body on this planet. This level is what will become the new "lightbody" of humanity.

Until now, all expansion into light beyond 73% had to take place in the upper realms, free of a physical form that could not sustain itself at a higher light quotient. As spontaneous combustion was not appealing, the great masters have known when they needed to move on. They have been able to surrender their human forms by allowing their physical bodies to die and the truth of their spiritual being to ascend, as with Yogananda.

The planet's frequency is now such that the transition into a body of Pure Light is becoming possible. No one knows how long it will be before anyone can increase their light to do this. However, we can all understand what a significant shift and accomplishment this will be for humanity.

This shift became possible when the conga line of humanity made its turn back toward the light. On December 16, 1994, the conga line reached its furthest point into the darkness and began its way home. People often ask, "Why that day?" Where were the stars, or what is the numerological significance? There was nothing mystical or pre-ordained about this date. That was just the day we arrived and turned around.

This information obviously cannot be verified scientifically. It is channeled. I know that many lightworkers who have been awake longer than I have been remember feeling a change in the planet's energy around that time. I know the truth in my heart is that this day did change the world. Does this date matter? No—it is just mental candy.

---

[28] Yogananda's death certificate can be found online. It states that he died of a heart attack. His heart just stopped. Some people use this to argue that he did not ascend but he merely died like all human beings. I am not sure any doctor, even a Hindu, is brave enough to give Ascension as the cause of death. This is only my opinion, of course.

Lightbody

What is a lightbody? Many people refer to one's auric field as the lightbody. Others reference the Tibetan Buddhist "rainbow body," the transition of the physical body into a body of light just before ascension, as the lightbody. In the future, the lightbody will be some beyond both of these.

Human history contains many stories of people who turned into light. The eastern cultures have hundreds of documented accounts and oral histories of spiritual masters transforming into bodies of light when their physical bodies die. The phenomenon is common among the Hindus and Buddhist masters but has also been noted numerous times in the Christian tradition. Some of the most extensive research on the rainbow body and other light phenomena has been conducted by Mitchell Earl Gibson, MD, and documented in his book *The Human Body of Light.*

However, the lightbody I am referring to is something new to this planet—a form that appears physical but is pure light. This body is beyond breatharian or the ability to sustain a physical body on air alone. A body of pure light needs no air, food, or water. So, how does it function?

From ancient times to only a few hundred years ago, a small group of priests has had the technology to create *ever-burning lamps*, sometimes referred to as perpetual or virgin lamps. The works of Rosicrucian scholar Hargrave Jennings and many others describe these lamps as found in temples and tombs, having burned for hundreds of years because the fuel never burns away. Several mystery schools had the technology to construct lamps that extracted energy from the atmosphere that continuously renewed the fuel supply. In other words, invisible energy was the resource for sustaining the physical lamps.

The new human lightbody will sustain itself entirely on invisible energy, like an ever-burning lamp. While no one on earth has achieved this yet, we are getting closer. When the first master performs this transformation, it will undoubtedly be exciting for all humanity.

The Conga Line Keeps Moving

Because the conga line was able to reverse its direction and begin moving all humanity back into the light, new energy channels have opened. These new channels allowed higher frequency techniques to become available to us. These techniques enable human beings to refine the healing process and move more quickly through the layers of separation than the masters who led us this far. Many of the symptoms of bringing in more light and releasing darkness will be less harsh than they have been in the past. That is very good news.

But, no matter what you experience, just keep going. Like Dory in the movie *Finding Nemo*, "Just keep swimming."[29] It does not matter where you are in the conga line. Some of us started sooner, and some of us began later. Either way, we all have to go through all the steps to get home. It is how the system works.

No one is dropping down from the sky to take you home. There is no growth and no mastery in being rescued. You are here to become a master. It is in your DNA. You just keep doing your process and following the roads you have designed for yourself. You just keep swimming.

While the Experiment in Duality is complete at the highest levels of consciousness, the process is not complete on earth. Life for humanity will go on as we wrap up the details. Those who do not reach the Fifth or Sixth Levels of Initiation in this life will come back and continue the journey with new bodies and new learning opportunities. We still have much to learn about duality and separation by completing our process. I, for one, do not want to waste my many lifetimes of learning by cutting the experiment short and missing out on living mastery.

Looking around the world, you might doubt that humanity has turned back toward the light. The high degree of turmoil and discord you see today does not indicate that things are moving in the wrong direction. It is an indication that things are moving in the right direction. You are seeing the side effects of our energetic cleansing.

---

[29] *Finding Nemo*, dir. by Andrew Stanton (2003; Walt Disney Productions and Pixar Animation Studios).

Anyone who has done an herbal or dietary cleanse to rid the body of toxins knows that releasing those old toxins creates some unpleasantness. As the toxins that have been held in the cells break loose, one may experience headaches, skin breakouts, diarrhea, aching joints and muscles, and more. The process can be downright uncomfortable, especially the first time through.

The release of old emotional, mental, and spiritual toxins is no different. As a human being's frequency goes higher, the toxins long held in the subconscious are forced to the surface, and the lower-self acts out. This cleansing can show up as weepiness, whining, irritation, short-tempers, and on down the scale to extreme violence. As the lower-self feels pushed to raise its frequency and let go of the old, it will fight to hold on to what it believes to be its power. The struggle is as unpleasant on the inside as it appears to be on the outside.

The healing process is not always pretty. Our goal is to make it as comfortable and joyful as possible, but we will all hit a few bumps along the way. Patience, compassion, and love are how we get through it ourselves and how we help others do the same.

The conga line will keep moving, and all of humanity will get through the final door. Those already at the college level on their spiritual road will get through sooner. Those still in the first grade of their journey will need more time before graduating.

As time goes on and more people move into higher levels of initiation, all of humanity will find it easier to let go of the old. The more role models we have at higher frequencies, the easier it will be for others to find someone to follow until they can stand on their own. We are Source. Let's remember now.

Chapter 10

Surrender and the Divine Plan

Once Jesus was asked by the Pharisees when the kingdom of God
was coming, and he answered,
"The kingdom of God is not coming with things that can be observed;
nor will they say, 'Look, here it is!' or
'There it is!' For, in fact, the kingdom of God is among you."
—Luke 17:20, *The NRSV Bible*

We are the creators. Everyone in metaphysics has heard this said over and over. Grasping what this means and balancing it with the Divine Plan for this universe can be a mystery and sometimes frustrating. The lower-self asks, "If I am the creator, why can't I create anything I want? Why do I have to consider a Divine Plan? Why do I have to go to my guidance? After all, I am God! Why can't I just have what I want?"

Good questions. Why can't we always have what we want? Why do we have to go to our guidance?

Once again, the answers to these questions lie in "it's not the what; it's the why." It is not what we want, but why we want it. Is what we want for the highest good of all, or is it merely ego gratification? Is what we desire even for our own highest good, or are we asking to eat the chocolate cake before dinner and then wondering why we don't want what is healthier for us? Are we coming from spiritual infancy, spiritual adolescence, or spiritual maturity?

None of this is easy. We have a huge learning curve to shift from who we have been inside the experiment and who we will be as spiritual masters. Moving from the old selfishness of separation into the selflessness of oneness is quite a leap.

Selflessness does not mean we have to do without. It means we need to look to the highest good, always coming from love without any intention that brings harm to others. Harm to others. What does that mean?

Here is when it can get tricky. We understand that making choices that intentionally harm others, such as trying to put someone out of business for personal gain, is not the way to oneness. However, what might appear harmful in 3rd-dimensional consciousness might be a perfect creation from the soul's perspective.

The road to Ascension winds us through our fears, anger, greed, self-pity, unworthiness, selfishness, and more. It must. We cannot graduate from this experiment without healing all the issues of separation. How do we heal if we do not have the opportunity to face our issues? How do we know if we are healed if we are never tested?

There is a great scene in the movie *Evan Almighty* from Universal Studios when God asks Joan, "If someone prays for patience, you think God gives them patience or does he give them the opportunity to be patient? If they prayed for courage, does God give them courage, or does he give them opportunities to be courageous? If someone prayed for the family to be closer, do you think God zaps them with warm, fuzzy feelings, or does he give them opportunities to love each other?"[30]

We may not always get what we ask for because it is not for our highest good. We may not get what we ask for because we are not yet ready. We might be guided to do something that we believe will hurt someone but is designed to give that someone an opportunity to learn, step out of their box, or step up to the plate. We do not always know what is in the highest good, but when we align with our souls and follow guidance, we will act for the highest good for ourselves and others.

---

[30] *Evan Almighty*, dir. by Tom Shadyak, (2007; Universal Pictures).

The Divine Plan

The Divine Plan is the universal plan for the highest good of the evolution of everything in the universe. The ultimate goal is to get everyone back into the light and on to the next stage of their growth.

The Divine Plan is an outline, with many contingency plans for how the goal might be achieved. We are in a free-will universe. Beings here have free choice in their experiences, and every choice can change the plan's direction.

The Divine Plan is not predestination. Predestination is the belief that a God outside of us has preordained—pre-decided—every step of our lives; therefore, we have no control. We may appear to have choices, but the choices have already been made for us.

The Divine Plan is no different than any business plan or timeline structure for any event. When we lay out a plan, we set the long-term goal and begin to work backward on what needs to happen to achieve the desired result on time. However, we do know that well-laid plans do go awry. This principle applies to the upper realms as well as our 3rd-dimensional world.

A smart business person pays attention to what happens daily in their business and industry. With the worldwide interconnection of goods and services, any event, local or international, may necessitate a change in the business plan to get ahead or possibly to survive. A good business plan is flexible. Anyone who blindly holds to what looked good yesterday without considering today's changes is very likely headed in the wrong direction.

Our Divine Plan, both individual and collective, can shift every day. The eventual result is still oneness and Ascension, but the road to getting there could develop a few potholes. A detour might be in order, or perhaps an entirely new route would be more desirable.

Flexibility and following guidance are always the answer. The lower-self cannot possibly know what is in the highest good. The lower-self has limited knowledge on the first floor of our spiritual skyscraper. By going to the soul in the penthouse, we have access to all we need. If we do not know our own highest good without going to our soul, how can we know what is in someone else's highest good? We cannot.

The Divine Plan is designed to bring each of us what we need at all times to find our way home. The only question is whether we are willing to listen and follow it.

Divine Surrender

Surrender is ultimately the key to everything. It is both our first and our last step in the process of ascension. We must have a certain level of surrender to consider ourselves spiritual beings versus only human beings. Each step of the journey requires another layer of surrender as we let go of more and more of the illusion in exchange for our spiritual truth.

Ultimately, we must surrender all we are as individuals to experience oneness and make the final Ascension. Nothing short of 100% surrender will get you there. Some years ago, I saw a documentary on a group of Buddhist priests in an eastern monastery. The part that made the most significant impression on me at that time was their attempt to ascend. A few priests went into a courtyard and began spinning. Spinning is a technique that has been used for thousands of years to allow one's frequency to lift out of the body to touch the divine. The goal for these priests was to spin out of their bodies to their final Ascension.

In their conscious hearts and minds, they felt ready to surrender and go home to the light. One by one, they fell unconscious to the ground, hoping they had left their bodies behind. However, one by one, they awoke to find themselves still here. The conscious surrender was not enough. Somewhere buried in the subconscious was some form of fear which held onto the 3rd-dimensional world as real.

Those fears are important. The tiniest fears will keep us in the illusion of separation and out of ultimate oneness. What keeps us attached to the physical world is based on our emotional attachments, not the material. Our emotional attachments and responses come from our false beliefs, beliefs developed through many lifetimes in the experiment. Until we have healed all the false beliefs in separation, we will continue to hold some level of fear. As long as we hold any fear, we are still part of the illusion.

Most people have heard the saying that FEAR is False Evidence Appearing Real. Inside the illusion, this is so very true. Nothing in the illusion of separation is true. However, we have done a fine job convincing ourselves that it is. These beliefs make it challenging to surrender to our divine truth, no matter how much we want to believe it in our conscious minds.

Divine Surrender is free of all fear. Like the Buddhist priests in the film, we must heal all our subconscious beliefs to make the *final* Ascension.

The Knowing of Truth

We each know the truth inside of us. It can be tough to admit the truth when it does not align with what the lower-self wants its reality to be, which is why so many of us fall short from time to time. However, if we are willing to peel back the layers of behaviors, emotions, and beliefs, we know the divine answers, whether we like them or not. Psychotherapy and spiritual facilitation are both about peeling away the layers of the illusion to find our divine truth.

If we are unwilling to know our truth, we are challenged to follow the Divine Plan. My students are often dismayed to hear me say that their souls do not want them to settle for being happy. Their souls want them to experience Pure Joy, overcome all fear and stress, and experience total bliss. We cannot do that sitting in our comfort zones and pandering to the lower-self. *This desire for us does not mean we are not supposed to be happy*! The spiritual process is not supposed to be one of suffering, but it is one of letting go of who we have been and stepping through our fears.

The divine truth is within you. Embrace it. Do not shy away from all that you are. Somewhere within, you know that you are Source. Allow yourself to feel it and remember it, and you will know your true power. Your only purpose in life is to reclaim your divine knowing of who you are as pure love—as Source.

Rejoice in the Plan You Have Chosen

Who chooses your plan? You do. You chose the basic outline before you came into this body, filling in the blanks as you go.

Before coming into any lifetime, you evaluate where you are in your overall ascension process and decide with your soul what would be most beneficial to you. You then pack your spiritual suitcases with the issues you want to work toward healing and the gifts and talents you can share with the world in the process. You also pack things you love to do for fun in each life.

Everything in your suitcase is geared toward healing separation, being of service, and enjoying the experience of being human. The specifics depend on where you are in the conga line, how fast you want to make the next leap in evolution, and who you have agreed to work with on your journey. There are no bad plans. Like the Carriage Trail I described at Moses Cone, we will all get to the top no matter which configuration of loops we take.

Once the basics have been decided, you select your gender, nationality, race, religion, family, and anything else that needs to be considered to give you the best opportunity to achieve the goals for each life. Whatever the details of the plan that you have chosen, you chose them to help you conquer the next phase of your illusion.

You chose your gender to help you with the male/female issues you needed to heal. You chose your family to help you heal your relationships with the God/Goddess and the Heavenly Hosts. You chose your nationality, race, religion, body size, and more to help you learn what you wanted to learn in each life. Instead of lamenting, criticizing, and judging what you have chosen, you are better served by exploring why you made these choices and rejoicing in your brilliance.

What better way to heal past life issues around a specific religion than to be born into that religion in this life and *not* like it? What better way to identify issues with the Mother/Father God than to have those issues mirrored by your physical parents? What better way to heal the fears of being seen than being born with a very large body that cannot be missed or a petite body that often gets ignored? This list goes on and on.

You made your choices wisely. There are no victims here. When you see perfection in your plan, you open yourself to healing and knowing your truth. When you see the divinity in *your* plan, you open yourself to seeing the divinity in the choices of others. You move away from the intolerance and criticism that come from judging what other people do with their lives. There are no wrong plans, only the experience gained from the outcomes.

But My Plan Did Not Work Out!

Humans tend to beat themselves up when things do not go as planned or when things do not work out "right." We sometimes hold ourselves to impossible standards. Those standards are usually based on 3rd-dimensional expectations instead of 5th-dimensional standards, which are totally different.

It is important to be working toward the Divine Plan. We each chose our basic plan to help us evolve. Each month, each week, and each day that we check with our souls on our long-term or short-term plan, we are given information based on where we are now and what we need to do to get where we need to go for the highest good. It is our choice whether we follow. Even when we do our best, we may not arrive at the final outer world goal. Whether we achieve that goal or not, the process of trying is what moves us forward on the inner. Each issue we heal, each fear we resolve, and each new skill we learn expands us and takes us higher in frequency and further down the road of ascension. When a plan does not work out, we return to our guidance and start in a new direction.

Teresa shared the following story in class when we were discussing attachment and judgment of outcomes.

> One afternoon, I came across a squirrel that had been hit by a car. It was cartoon-flat like Wile E. Coyote after the anvil dropped on him while chasing the Road Runner—perfectly flat like a pressed flower. I immediately felt a wash of sorrow for the

> little guy, how his life had ended so callously on the pavement. Just as my sadness and outrage at this injustice began to grow, a loud, clear voice popped into my head, "Yeah, that did not go as planned."
>
> It was the squirrel's spirit. Rather than feeling sad, he was amused by the whole event. His experience was just, oops! Animals pop in and out of lifetimes quickly, with less attachment to bodies than we humans. That little squirrel, flat and dead as he was, showed me how to laugh a little at our attachment to form and our sadness about death, which, after all, is only a transformation, not an ending.

Sometimes we hit the mark, and sometimes we don't. Sometimes we arrive on time, and sometimes we are late. Sometimes we get what we expect, and sometimes we are caught off guard. Sometimes we get across the road, and sometimes we do not. That is how it goes, and it is how we learn. As the French say, *c'est la vie.*

The universe is full of plans and contingency plans. At this writing, we have over eight billion individual plans on earth that must fit into the Divine Plan for all of Earth and humanity. Each planet and star is the same. The plans for individual planets and stars must fit into the Divine Plan for the entire universe, and the plan for this universe must fit into the plan for the multi-universes.

We are the creators of our lives, but we are also co-creating with everyone else. Each day, someone makes a choice that could affect the plan for their family, country, planet, or universe. The Divine Plan's goal is to move everyone and everything into higher levels of light. The Divine Plan has a structure, but we create the details. The plans that do not "work out" are every bit as beneficial as the ones we believe do work out.

Flow depends on flexibility. Out of flexibility comes creativity. Out of creativity comes a new version of the plan. New plans are great because they show that we have moved into new areas of learning and healing. Rejoice in what seem to be your mistakes. They are blessings and guide you to where you need to go next.

Being of Service

We each have a form of service that goes to the foundation of our unique expression as Source. We chose our service before coming into this life to bring us joy and serve others. Some of us will bring that vision into form, and others will not this time around. Those who do find their chosen path and can pursue it with passion will find themselves zooming down the road of evolution and helping many others along the way.

Enlightened beings are needed in all areas of life for a community to thrive. We need farmers and mechanics, builders and inventors, artists and artisans, healers and teachers, administrators and council members, and more. All forms of service are valuable, and all forms of service are a path to ourselves-as-Source. The desire to be of service and to follow the path we have designed for ourselves is more important than achieving the outer world goals. We are seeking higher consciousness, not the ego gratification of outer world accomplishments.

Selfless service has been taught as a path to Ascension since the beginning of spiritual life on this planet. In 3rd-dimensional consciousness, the goal is to profit from service. In 5th-dimensional consciousness, the goal is to serve without regard for reward. This concept does not mean we are *not* rewarded for our service. Spirit has never intended that we starve our way to salvation because we cannot earn a livelihood using our gifts. It does mean that we must look to our inner motivations relative to our spiritual growth and why we do what we do. It's not the what; it's the why.

We cannot evaluate success on the spiritual path by what transpires on the outer, only by what happens on the inner. How do we know how well we are doing? We ask our souls. We must let go of outer world goals because they are the illusion. We must look at what is happening with our frequency, which may or may not be easy to evaluate. The lower-self might be feeling good because it has recognized a change in frequency, or it might be feeling good because it has been seduced by ego-gratification. The lower-self might get lost from time to time, but the soul always knows the highest plan and exactly how we are doing on our journey.

Getting the Vision and Working the Plan

One of the most important aspects of our spiritual evolution is clear channeling to our guidance, ourselves-as-Source. Accurate channeling requires practice and the ability to quiet the mind. When you can be still and clearly hear the inner voice of your soul, you are never lost, never without a plan, and never without guidance on the execution of that plan.

The purpose of getting the plan from your soul is to align with your highest good and the highest good of everyone concerned. The lower-self usually thinks it knows the highest good based on the 3rd-dimensional world standards. It wants safety, security, and abundance. If the lower-self does not know what is in its highest good in the 3rd dimension, it can't know the highest good in the 5th dimension.

By going to guidance, you can access the highest levels of the plan and get the most appropriate action steps for achieving the plan. You can get a long-term vision of the inner and the outer. You can get the steps needed today to make that vision come into form. This format is no different than creating and working a 3rd-dimensional plan except that it comes from your soul and allows you to focus on how the plan furthers your spiritual growth, not just your lower-self's desires.

And, most of the time, your soul's vision is much cooler than what the lower-self wants. Your soul knows the endless possibilities and your unlimited potential. The lower-self too often creates from lack, limitation, and what is expected. Opening to the Divine Plan is opening to your soul.

You must acknowledge that the lower-self will not always like the plan. You are often guided to do things your lower-self does not want to do but are required for your growth. Spiritual evolution requires letting go of the old. To move into higher levels of consciousness, you must face and heal all fears. You must let go of everything that holds you back.

The highest plan is not about things in the outer world. It is always for your spiritual evolution, inner growth, and healing. It is also for the highest good of the others who are cocreating the plan with you. Remember the hologram and how we help each other heal.

But What about the Others?

We are often concerned about how others might be affected by what we are guided to do. If we have asked for the Divine Plan, the plan for the highest good of all, we must trust that we are being guided for everyone's benefit. The highest plan is always for everyone's highest good.

We each need a variety of experiences to grow to our full potential as spiritual beings. Sometimes those experiences make the lower-self happy, and sometimes they do not. Just as for human children growing up, some of the most valuable lessons on our road to Ascension come through hard knocks and tough love. When we embrace what we call the bad along with the good, we progress much faster and can find joy in every moment, no matter what.

As individuals, we do not know what someone else needs to learn to evolve. However, their soul knows. The lower-self often believes it knows what is in someone else's highest good, but it does not know more than that person's soul! We have to act with trust and surrender if we truly desire to be of service to ourselves and others.

Everyone has their path based on their spiritual suitcase. Just as someone else cannot do your ascension for you, you cannot do it for someone else. I always set the intention to move through my evolution with divine grace, ease, and joy. No matter what I have left to learn or to heal, I want to do it with as much fun and laughter as possible. I hold that intention for everyone in my life, but I am not in charge of making that happen. They are the creators of their lives, and I can only ride along, observe, and support them.

Remembering that we are all creating our illusion for what we need is important. When we focus on the circumstances instead of the purpose, we get sucked into the dread instead of remaining in the light. In the 3rd dimension, we say, live and let live. Metaphysically, we could say, evolve and let evolve. Learn to rejoice in the plan you have chosen and in the plans others have chosen. It is all good.

One of the greatest things any of us can do is to model the divine in us at all times. If we want to help others, we first need to help ourselves.

Master the teachings and walk through life with joy in your heart. Share that with others during their hard times and help others evolve by demonstrating what you know.

Surrendering When the Plan Changes

The Divine Plan is designed to bring us back into the full remembrance of who we are as Source. The Law of Attraction tells us that within, so without—that like energy attracts like energy. The Divine Plan changes as energy changes. As we change and the world around us changes, our plans must shift to correspond to the new frequency. Flexibility is essential to harmony. Detachment is essential to peace.

This book has been some time in the making. I had it almost complete for publication in 2009. I was falling behind the schedule I had received from my guidance, and I could feel the energy shifting.

During June and July 2010, I experienced a significant personal jump in my frequency. I had put the book aside to focus on integrating these changes and working on some other items. In August of that year, I was told by my soul that it was no longer the highest plan to finish the book at this time. I was to change the direction of what I was doing. This change was in perfect divine order for several reasons and served me well. In 2013, I was led to rewrite and publish the first edition of the book. I am now in the third version. Each time I am guided to review and republish this book, the frequency goes higher.

The purpose of following the highest plan is to help us evolve. The outer world significance is minor compared to inner growth. If the plan is no longer serving our highest good, we will be guided to make a change.

I had dawdled on my timeline for the book. I had changed so significantly that finishing and promoting the book would have slowed my process instead of accelerating it. The world was changing such that what I had to share would be better modified and saved for another time.

The changes within me and the world were no excuse for missing my timeline. I had to simply acknowledge that if I had completed the original book on time, my path would have moved in one direction, but it was now moving in another direction that would serve me just as well. Our souls have multiple contingency plans for our evolution, and my plan had changed based on my choices and my shift in frequency. It was time to allow and detach—free of judgment and free of self-recrimination. I think the book is better now than the version I first wrote. I have been able to add, delete, and massage the content for who I am today and who my readers are today. I am very happy about that.

Whatever changes we need to make in the Divine Plan, for whatever reason, should be embraced for what we have learned and where those changes will take us. One of the biggest reasons our plan changes is that we have outgrown it. This shift is a cause for celebration, not regret. Being in the flow depends on the willingness to let go. If we cannot let go when the time comes, we will stay stuck in the illusion of duality.

It Is Always Simple, but It Is Not Always Easy

The Divine Plan is always in everyone's highest good, no matter how the outer world may look. If we are truly clear when we get our guidance, we know that we are acting for everyone's spiritual expansion.

However, that is not always easy. The 3rd-dimensional paradigm, as we know it, is going through its death phase. As the experiment ends, the lower-self and all the old-world systems are also coming to an end. It will not always be easy to watch what is happening during this transition or to allow others to move through it in their way without interfering.

Plan A is always Ascension, no matter how we get there. We must take responsibility for whatever road we choose. We must also allow others to take responsibility for their choice of paths as well. Some of us are making that road easier for ourselves, and others are making it more difficult.

Choosing to make the road easy requires the resolve to let go of all emotional attachments and responsibility for others. When faced with difficult choices in the 3rd-dimensional world, we often hear someone say, "It's complicated," or, "It's not that easy." We know it is *not complicated.* That person just does not like their choices. Perhaps they are concerned about their personal comfort zone. Perhaps they are concerned about what other people may think. Perhaps they are afraid of hurting someone else or any number of other emotional outcomes.

When we are clearly guided, the choices are straightforward. When we can allow and detach, the choices are also easy.

Non-attachment is a step-by-step process. Ending the illusion of duality necessitates total non-attachment to everything inside the illusion. This concept is foreign to the lower-self, who sees non-attachment as non-caring. Divine detachment centers on love, understanding, and compassion for another's circumstances. Divine love, understanding, and compassion are based on knowing that we are each creating our own experiences for our evolution. We need to empower others to make their choices and learn from the experiences they are creating, just as we are learning from ours.

We climb the staircase of human frequencies to our spiritual mastery over time. As we climb higher, our wisdom expands, and everything gets clearer and easier. I promise.

Oneness with Source

Surrender to the Divine Plan is surrender to oneness with Source. Surrender to the Divine Plan is our ultimate destiny if we are to end the Experiment in Duality and fully realize ourselves as Source. The Divine Plan is our ultimate empowerment because it allows us to see ourselves as part of All That Is and feel our total unlimitedness. Holding on to the old ways and the old visions keeps us from our truth and our graduation to the next realm of mastery.

Surrender is both exciting and frightening. It is both exhilarating and debilitating. We long to know the unconditional love of Source and our divine power. We want to remember where we came from and who we are. We want to know the feeling of oneness again. At the same time, reaching that place in our evolution requires so many changes and so much letting go that the lower-self can sometimes feel overwhelmed and even paralyzed, like the proverbial deer in headlights.

We find the answer to this dilemma in trusting and focusing on love. Remember those glorious, love-filled experiences in life and meditation when your connection to Source is too strong to be denied when the process gets challenging. Rise above the outer world to observe the illusion as your soul observes it. Feel the awe, wonder, fascination, and amazement at all that is happening. And above all, focus on love.

Keep climbing the staircase one step and one octave at a time. Remember, we cannot do this wrong. We can only do it with more joy or less joy. The level of joy we experience is a matter of our perspective. Feel the oneness with All That Is—with the perfection of the journey and divinity of each experience. I once heard Jim Rohn say, "Don't get frustrated; get fascinated!"[31]

[31] Jim Rohn was an American entrepreneur, author, and motivational speaker who died on Dec. 5, 2009.

Chapter 11

Climbing the Staircase

Mere philosophy will not satisfy us. We cannot reach the goal by mere words alone. Without practice, nothing can be achieved.
—Sri Swami Satchidananda, *The Yoga Sutras of Patanjali*

In the passage above, Sri Swami Satchidananda explains the founding principle of all spiritual practices. Ascension, raising our frequency and healing our darkness, does not have to be difficult. We may believe it is complicated and tend to make it so. But all it requires is consistent and persistent practice and attention to detail.

Throughout this book, I have spoken of mastery versus divine mastery. However, the shift from lower levels of mastery to divine mastery does not happen by whim or fancy. We are all spiritual masters at some level of our being and experience. Our knowledge is in our DNA.

One of the great paradoxes of evolution is that we have to *do* something to experience our full spiritual nature. We are indeed "human beings, not human doings." It is true that "all of our answers are inside of us." That does not mean we have nothing to do.

For example, westerners often misunderstand the Daoist teaching that all we have to do is to be. Some people have taken this to mean that we move through our lives, and everything will fall into place. The Daoists are very thoughtful about what unfolds in their lives. They take life into their hearts, meditate, and contemplate. One merely has to visit a Daoist temple or training center to see that much is being done—specific meditations and Daoist exercises, Qigong, and other spiritual activities. The paradox is that we must *do things* to learn how to *just be.*

In this final chapter, I am giving ten recommendations for climbing the spiral staircase to Ascension. While each road to the Buddha will have its specific process, the ten recommendations below encompass a large percentage of what everyone needs to ascend. Go to your guidance to evaluate what you need and how well you may already be doing in these areas. Then ask your self-as-Source how you are to proceed. It is your creation.

Ten Recommendations for Climbing the Staircase

1. Learn to meditate.

Meditation is essential to any spiritual practice. Mastering a quiet physical, emotional, and mental body is key to oneness. Without a state of total quiet, one cannot fully experience the realm beyond the physical.

A true state of meditation is the state of total quiet. Many exercises are called meditations, but they are techniques to get one into a quiet state. Guided meditations, staring at candles, chanting, and others are methods to get the lower bodies to relax and let go, not the meditation itself. If one has not achieved the state of mindlessness, one has not reached the full meditative state.

The Buddha said there would come a time when we had no thoughts. This saying is taught throughout the Eastern practices and was a fundamental principle in all Middle Eastern mystery schools and early Christianity. Until the "monkey mind" is quiet, one cannot hear the Word of God.

Western man prides himself on his intellect. The last thing the western mental body wants to do is to be quiet. It does not want to give up what it believes to be its power to figure out things, organize, create, and be in control. A true state of meditation is the surrender of all lower bodies to the experience of oneness.

I have had many students over the years who resisted meditation but can now hardly wait for their meditation time. The joy in the connection to our truth, power, and place in the universe gained through meditation cannot be equaled by anything in the outer world illusion. It just takes practice.

2. Learn to be a clear channel.

Channeling is often misunderstood. A channel is just an open line of communication. Just as a radio or TV network sends signals through a radio or TV channel in the 3rd-dimensional world, the universe is one giant communication network with many channels to which we can connect. The most important channel is the one from our souls. A clear connection to ourselves-as-Source is how we know what is truly in our highest good and how to proceed without giving away our power.

The emphasis is on *clear*. Anyone can learn to channel. While many people are born with their psychic skills functioning, most of us need to learn how to develop our abilities. The most important aspect of channeling is understanding when one is clearly connected and when one is not. We can channel our lower-selves so that we only hear what we want to hear. We can filter what we hear from a higher source through our lower-frequency beliefs and desires, distorting the message.

Channeling is not difficult to learn. The more significant challenge is learning to discern your level of clarity. As with all the things you need to practice, there are a wide variety of techniques. Find a good teacher who focuses on being 100% clear and has a method that feels comfortable.

Until you learn to channel your soul, you will be seeking wisdom from the outside rather than from the inside. Therefore, you will be giving away your power. Becoming a clear channel is essential to mastering the Third Level of Initiation and the upper levels of an avatar. Once again, this does not mean you do not still seek out teachers. Until you are 100% clear 100% of the time, you may need help. Masters know when to stand on their own and trust themselves and when to ask for help by balancing confidence and humility.

Helen has been strongly intuitive her entire life. She knows to trust and follow. However, she had an experience that showed the true power of her interconnectedness and the importance of listening to her guidance. Here is her story.

> After accepting a position in Washington State, I was there for a house-hunting trip and stayed at a local inn. The ferry to Whidbey Island was next door. Partway into my trip, I "heard" I was supposed to go to the island.
>
> When I departed the ferry, I saw several buses at the dock on Whidbey. I heard from guidance to take the third bus in line. There wasn't any place to put coins, and I didn't have a bus pass. I asked the driver where I was supposed to put my money and how much it was. "The bus is free today," he said. I was the only passenger on that bus.
>
> The bus driver was very happy and cheerful. He drove for about 20 minutes, telling me about the island. We stopped in front of a boardwalk, which had rows of shops. He told me I could catch the bus back to the ferry every hour from that stop.
>
> I departed the bus and started walking the boardwalk. I saw a shop with plus-size clothing advertised and a beautiful scarf in the window. I walked into the shop, and immediately my hair was on fire (my signal that something important is about to happen).
>
> I didn't see any clothing as advertised, but I saw pictures of ascended masters everywhere. I was a bit confused. I asked the woman behind the counter where the clothes were. She said the clothes weren't there yet, but did I want to look at a scarf? As I looked at the scarf, the woman asked if I was Helen, and I said yes. She told me, "We have been waiting for you. I am so happy you have arrived."
>
> That was an A-HA moment for me. We talked for a while. When we finished with why I was there, I left (without a scarf) and went to wait for the bus. My head and body were

buzzing like a transmission line. I wasn't sure what had just happened.

Sure enough, a bus picked me up—the same bus and driver. The driver mentioned that I wasn't carrying any shopping bags. I told him I guessed I wasn't there to shop but to learn.

3. Go into the silence.

Going into "the silence" is not the same as meditating. Although the goal is to achieve silence in meditation, going into the silence means spending time without speaking, free of outside noise and interference. The necessity of this experience is also part of every solid spiritual process.

The sounds of a human voice and the modern mechanical and electronic world are energetically distracting and mentally stimulating. Working on a project, contemplating an idea, listening to music, and reading (even journaling) involve the lower bodies. These activities keep you in the illusion of the physical. The purpose of going into the silence is to reach a mindless state while consciously in the body—to have no thoughts.

My husband and I met a man in the canyons of Utah who explained it perfectly. He had been going to the desert alone for years. His friends could not understand why he would do that and how he could not be bored to tears.

He would tell them, "When you first start, it is uncomfortable. You want someone else to talk with. But you get to be okay talking to yourself. Eventually, you realize that talking to yourself is really boring, so you stop. Then, there is just perfect silence. You cannot explain perfect silence, but once you have it, you want it again." I cannot say it better than he did.

Many Hindu, Buddhist, Christian, and Jewish facilities offer time and space for silent retreats. Some offer special programs, and some simply offer rooms to those who want to get away from the outer world. I know only two people who are successful with silent retreats at home. Not many people can face the challenge of turning off all electronics (TV, radio, phones, computers, etc.) and not being drawn into the projects that need to get done. People often feel embarrassed to tell others they will be home but don't call. If other people live in the house, they must also participate in the silence, which means no conversations, no eye contact, and no hanky-panky.

Going to an appropriate facility or renting a cabin for a few days will be beneficial. For many people, one day in silence seems almost more than they can stand. But holding out for two, if not three, days will pay off. Even if you cannot maintain perfect silence for that long, and even if you do not reach an entirely quiet mind the first time, it will be a success. As with everything I recommend, practice. Just repeat and repeat until you understand and appreciate the blissful state of a quiet mind.

4. Remember, this is an illusion, and you are the creator.

Nothing in the physical world is real, so do not give it power. With the full understanding that everything is energy and that energy is moved by intention, the power to create through your thoughts and focus becomes quite clear. What you believe and how you focus your intention does create your reality. Whether looking at an individual creation or a co-creation, you are the power inside your illusion.

As your frequency increases and you gain confidence in your psychic abilities, seeing the physical world as the illusion gets easier. The first time this came fully home for me was my first big "you cannot possibly doubt this" clairvoyant experience.

I was teaching a series of classes in Pennsylvania in 2002. On one of our days off, a friend and I went to Philadelphia for a day of sightseeing. It was raining, and we sat on a downtown bench under our umbrellas, waiting for a trolley. As I sat watching strangers walk by on the busy street, I suddenly no longer saw people. I only saw outlines of human forms with beautiful white lights, like lanterns, in the center of their chests. The physical world had vanished. All separation had been dissolved and washed away.

I had had experiences with my clairvoyant skills for some time, but nothing like this. Not only had I never seen such an all-encompassing vision, I had never felt such a connection to people I did not know and would probably never see again. The way I see the physical world has been different ever since.

In *Autobiography of a Yogi*, Yogananda described having a similar experience with the assistance of his great guru, Sri Yukteswar[32]. Whatever your first complete encounter with the invisible truth may be, do not brush it aside. Do not let it go. Integrate and assimilate it. Let it grow until you have mastered it as your reality and the creative energy that flows from it.

5. Stop beating up the "ego."

The "ego" is not bad. The ego has been defined in many ways for many years. Moving the term ego from psychology into metaphysics, the ego-self is what I refer to in my practice as the lower-self. The lower-self is the lower three bodies of who we are as human beings—the physical, emotional, and mental self.

While the lower-self must be healed to move back into oneness, it is not, and never has been, "bad." The lower bodies believe themselves separate from Source because we did an excellent job creating the illusion. The lower-self was expected to act in separation until it could understand how to come back into oneness. It was part of the original plan.

We heal the lower-self (the ego-self) with love. We must *love* the lower-self into alignment with the soul before it can trust the soul. Blaming the ego, punishing the ego, or pushing away the ego creates more separation and makes healing more difficult.

Think of the ego as a lost and terrified child. This child finally sees the door to its home only to find the one who is supposed to love it most, screaming that it is unworthy, the source of all the trouble, and should be silent and go away.

Beating up the ego starts with blame at the First Level of Initiation but is still strongly present in lightworkers at the third level. We cannot heal ourselves when we are busy beating ourselves up, and beating up the ego *is* beating ourselves up. We cannot, nor should we, try to separate our ego

---

[32] Paramahansa Yogananda, *Autobiography of a Yogi*, 13th edition, The International Publications of Self-Realization Fellowship, Los Angeles, CA, 1998.

from who we are as Source. It is an integral part of this creation and our unique expression of ourselves as Source.

Forgiveness begins with self-forgiveness, which means forgiveness of what we call the ego. Like the Prodigal Son, the ego-self must feel it is safe to come home. It must feel safe to move back into oneness. We must embrace all parts of ourselves to heal ourselves.

6. Get past all dogma.

Dogma can be present in all spiritual practices. It is not limited to institutionalized religions. If you are paying attention, you will hear dogma from the followers of the "churches" *and* those who have moved into other spiritual practices. I have encountered dogma in every version of spirituality, from religion to New Age to atheism.

What is dogma, and what is not? Dogma is an authoritarian set of principles. Someone is saying there is only one truth, which is this one. All spiritual philosophies and practices have sets of principles and guidelines. They must have to convey the message. The authoritarian and indisputable aspects of the teachings turn philosophy into dogma.

The great masters shared divine truth with their students to the best of their ability, free of dogma. Once the masters were gone, their students did their best to relay the message. However, the message often became disjointed, misunderstood, and dogmatized over time.

This concept applies to any practice or organization that feels it has all the answers. It applies to atheists who are as dogmatic about believing there is no God as the "believers" they rail against. Eight billion people can have seven billion different truths. You need to open your heart and allow others to be who they are and believe what they believe at any point in their lives. You must also allow this for yourself.

Healing dogma is not as easy as it would seem. To heal all your layers of dogma, you must be aware of the following subtle forms of dogma.

- Silent dogma—that which you hear rolling around in your head but do not voice because it would not seem spiritual.

- Subconscious dogma—that which you do not even recognize you have.
- Judgments you do not consider dogma—but are.
- Attachments to what the lower-self wants to believe versus the discernment of your soul—not allowing your truth to change.

All forms of dogma create separation. Each of these subtle forms can last well into the upper frequencies of the Third Level of Initiation and the lower frequencies of the fourth level. They must all be healed for Ascension. Time, patience, and awareness will get you there.

The most important energy to heal is judgment. Judgment creeps into every area of human life. When you are free of all judgment, you have no attachment, fear, need to prove or defend yourself, and, therefore, no dogma. There are no rights or wrongs, only differences.

7. Heal your beliefs about karma and all other religious influences.

The vast majority of humanity misunderstands the principle of karma. Karma is the principle that like energy attracts like energy. Who we are on the inner is what we attract on the outer.

The saying "what goes around comes around" has led to the belief that someone in the heavens keeps a cosmic balance sheet of rewards and punishments due to us based on our outer world behaviors. However, our karma is simply the energies that we hold. These energies do not have to be played out in the physical world unless we leave them unhealed. If we hold anger, we create from anger. If we hold self-pity, we create from self-pity, and so on. When we heal these issues, our creations change.

There was a time on the planet when the only way to move through our old energies was by overcoming them through the physical world experience. No more. There is nothing that we cannot heal energetically. When we change our inner energies, we change our karma and, therefore, what we create.

The concepts that we have to "pay back," "be punished for," or "make amends for" the past are major blocks to oneness and Ascension. The opposite belief that we are "entitled to," "owed for," or should "be rewarded for" our good deeds also take away our power. We are the creators and must accept all we create has a purpose. Our creations are the mirrors of what we have healed and what we have not. Nothing more.

Karmic beliefs run very deep. Most people consciously and subconsciously believe in the need to pay back our debts, not only the need to pay back people we think we've harmed, but also all of humanity, Mother Earth, and Source. The time and energy spent trying to pay for our sins are much better spent healing our guilt and shame and knowing ourselves as divine love. The Lords of Karma (the ascended masters who are the Karmic Board members) have been telling humanity for decades to let go of the old views of karma. It is time just to be love.

We have all had many past lives under many religious structures. All the limiting beliefs from all religions need to be healed. It does not have to be difficult. We merely need to be aware and ask to let go.

This understanding is more important than most people think. If you have any judgment toward any religion, especially the one into which you chose to be born, those judgments and beliefs must be healed. No one was dropped in here against their will. You are the creator. Whatever religious background you chose for this life, you decided with purpose. Use that. Heal that and know yourself as one.

Every religion has a set of rewards and punishments. Whether those beliefs follow some version of heaven and hell or a karmic balance sheet, the underlying principle is the same. Do good things and expect to be rewarded. Do bad things and expect to be punished.

All of this is based on outer world behavior without thought to the inner being. We cannot heal permanently by manipulating the illusion and doing things on the outer. We can only heal permanently by surrendering on the inner. Remember divine justice and the story of the Prodigal Son. Just forgive, love, and go home.

8. Learn to balance your life.

A spiritually balanced life focuses on three categories with the emphasis on spiritual evolution. They are (1) self, (2) service, and (3) family and friends. The ultimate balance for someone in a physical body is an equal amount of time and energy spent in each of the three categories.

This format is not the standard American lifestyle and probably not the norm in more than a small number of monasteries and indigenous cultures worldwide. Most people are pushed to earn a livelihood, take care of family, and maybe have a little time left for themselves. I have met very few people who feel they live a balanced life.

We are very unlikely to achieve perfect balance each day. The goal is to maintain our balance over a week or a month. Many people have found out, "If I don't maintain my balance, the universe may take care of it for me!"

Everything that we do as human beings falls into one of these areas. Sometimes the categories overlap, and sometimes they must stand alone. No one needs to get a ruler and a calculator to determine their balance. We each have our guidance for that. We do, however, need to understand the categories.

The first and most important of the three is the self. Self is the most difficult of the three for most people to accept. We have so many things we *have* to do. We have so many obligations and things that are expected of us.

I remember driving down a Georgia highway in my twenties and seeing a billboard that said:

J = Jesus first
O = others next
Y = yourself last

I remember thinking how sad to believe that God wanted us to have little or nothing left for ourselves. That was not the way I read the teachings of Jesus.

We have been raised to believe it is selfish to put ourselves first when it is the opposite. There is a good reason why a flight attendant says, "In case of emergency, put on *your* oxygen mask first. Then help others around you." If you pass out or die from a lack of oxygen, you cannot help anyone, including your children. You might even create problems for the other passengers.

If we do not take care of ourselves physically, emotionally, mentally, and spiritually, we do not have the energy or the focus to be of service to others. If we do not take care of ourselves, we are desecrating the lives and bodies we have chosen for our spiritual paths.

Life is meant to be enjoyed. We need to nurture ourselves if we are also to nurture others. It means taking care of our bodies. It means getting enough rest and enough exercise. It means doing things that bring us joy and renewal. Above all, it means creating time for meditation and other spiritual pursuits on our road to Ascension.

The second category is service. For most people, this means a job. That job might be income-earning, homemaking, or volunteer work. As we move into more awareness of ourselves as spiritual beings, the focus of service shifts emphasis from income and what others might expect of us to spiritual service, the divine service discussed in Chapter 9. A winning moment comes when we can earn a livelihood using the skills we packed in this life's spiritual suitcase. It will not happen for everyone, but that is all right. Joy and balance can still be found. Just trust guidance.

The third category is family and friends. Some categories overlap, which means that sometimes the energy in the category of self might also fall into time with family and friends. The challenge is that everyone in this category only gets one-third of our time—combined. Our spouse, children, parents, and friends all fit here. It is more doable for most people than we might think. We simply have to learn when to let go.

How does this breakdown in hours per day or week? Begin with the number of hours you sleep. First, ask your soul if you are getting too much or too little sleep and make any adjustments first. No excuses.

The remaining hours are divided by three. For example, if you are in bed for nine hours on average, you have fifteen hours remaining each day or 5 hours each day for each category. This plan does not fit the schedules of many people. However, look at these numbers weekly instead of daily; you have thirty-five hours for each of the three categories. This plan is manageable.

Can't get your boss to agree to a thirty-five-hour workweek? It is not yet a perfect world for creating perfect spiritual balance. The point is to get started and make changes where you can. The only way to successfully transition from where you are now to the balance that is in your highest good is to go to your soul for guidance. I make no apologies for how many times I have said to go to your guidance. Connecting to your soul is where you find your truth and your power.

When I began this process, my life was about 20% in balance. I had to start making tough choices, trading one activity for another. For many years now, I have lived in close to perfect spiritual balance. It can be done, and the feeling is quite incredible. The peace, ease, and expansion of a balanced life must be experienced to be appreciated. The typical 3rd-dimensional schedule will not bring bliss or allow time for a more rapid spiritual evolution. Begin exploring your daily plan with your soul and see what choices you have.

I mentioned earlier, "If I don't maintain my balance, the universe may take care of it for me." I have had many students share stories of ignoring their guidance on changing their plans and letting go of activities that no longer served them. When small consequences were not enough to get their attention, they manifested illnesses, broken arms, wrecked cars, and more. If you are choosing your spiritual path, follow it! Walk the talk and take command of your life as the spiritual being that you are. Remember that the physical world is an illusion.

9. Balance your male and female energies.

We are both male and female. The creation of a human body requires the merging of the male sperm and the female egg. We get our genetic traits from both parents, even though we have a physical gender. Our brains have left and right lobes, which are our male and female ways of thinking. We have the male energy of the nervous system and the female energy of the circulatory system. When our physical male and female energies are aligned and balanced, we have physical health and balanced thinking.

Our spiritual genetics are the same. We have both the male and female creative energies within us—the God and Goddess aspects of Source. To find our spiritual balance, we must balance our inner male and female. These archetypes must be healed and merged back into harmony, cooperation, unity, and oneness to know ourselves as Source and achieve Ascension. We must love and nurture them both, understand that they are both important, and honor them equally. If we do not, we cannot find balance, which means we cannot find true peace.

In Chapter 6, I described the female as the "being" state, the state in which ideas are born and nurtured to become clear intentions for creation. The male is the "action" state, the movement of energy to bring the intentions into form. Both are essential for creation, and both are essential for spiritual harmony.

One of the ancient creation stories says that God sent forth energy and created the earth and its creatures. However, God and the beings He had created were so far apart in frequency that they could not understand each other. God was impatient with humanity, and humanity was afraid of God. Source then created Wisdom to sit between the two. She taught God how to have compassion for humanity, and she taught humanity not to fear God.

The action state alone is heartless. The feeling state alone is mindless. The two must be blended and used in balance to experience the divine.

Begin a self-exploration of your inner male and female. Take notice of when you are using your male energy and when you are using your female. It takes practice. We are so programmed to see ourselves as male or female by gender that the ability to view ourselves as both takes time. The longer we delay this part of evolution, the more painful it can become. The inner male and female long for reunification. Get started today!

10. Accept that there is no single "spiritual" diet.

That is right. There is no spiritual diet. There is only what your body needs at any time for its health and ability to hold more light.

Diet might not seem a hot topic for moving into Ascension, but I find many lightworkers struggling with health choices: meat or no meat, vegetarian or vegan, raw or cooked, gluten-free, dairy-free, or breatharian (no food at all). There is no one answer. We are unique individuals with different needs at different times.

The Standing in the Light® program emphasizes channeling clearly to our souls. In the channeling class, we use simple questions for practice, like what is in my highest good to eat for dinner. Over the years, I have had many surprised, even shocked, vegetarian students who were guided to go out for chicken, fish, or, heaven forbid, a steak.

Before I go further, I am very careful about my diet. I pay attention to what I put in my body. I do my best to get high-quality, high-frequency food (organic whenever possible) and trust my guidance on what I need to eat for my highest good. At this writing, I am about 95% vegetarian. However, I have been in and out of vegetarianism and meat-eating throughout my twenty-five years of serious spiritual pursuit. What is right for me might not be right for you.

It is not the food we choose, but why we choose it. Our bodies have a wide variety of needs, which will change as we transition through various levels of light. If you have been convinced that a specific way to eat is the only healthy way or the only spiritual way to eat, I recommend getting into a good meditative state and checking with your soul whether it is best for you now. If it is right for you, great. If it is not, change.

For example, you might have chosen vegetarianism based on the belief that it is ungodly to eat animal flesh and inhuman to kill for food. However, consider that plants are also living beings that we kill for food. Many scientific studies show that plants are fully connected to their surroundings and feel pain. It is not that we take plants or animals for sustenance. It is the intention, reverence, and gratitude with which we do it. Looking to "it's not the what; it's the why," you can ask if you are making your choices based on your judgments or for your highest good. Your soul has the answers that are right for you.

I am not giving anyone *carte blanche* on their food choices. I am recommending that you follow your guidance at all times and do whatever is needed to prepare your body for holding the higher frequencies. As we move higher in frequency, we need more calcium and magnesium. We need more adenosine triphosphate (try lemons and limes). We need more protein (plant or animal). We need easily digestible, nutrient-dense foods.

It is possible to survive on no food, which is called breatharian. Becoming breatharian is not a requirement for Ascension. Many people are pursuing survival on air alone, but the question is, why? If this is your path, your soul will know and prepare you for this transition. However, too many people have been trying to push their bodies where they are not prepared to go and paying a heavy price. The key point is that Ascension is an innerworld project. You cannot *do* it through the outer world illusion. Your soul will let you know if your body is ready for vegetarian, vegan, raw, or other. Trust and follow.

Conclusion

There are many roads to the Buddha. My recommendation is only one. Buddha taught, “If you meet me on the road, kill me. Kill me immediately, for I am not the Buddha. You are the Buddha.” Buddha, Master Jesus, Krishna, and all the truly great masters have known themselves to be teachers of divine truth and leaders of the way home, not saviors. None of them have wanted to take our power. They have only aimed to empower us. All courses of study are just that—only courses of study. None of them has the only answer or is the only way. This one is no different.

I have studied many roads to Ascension to get to where I am now on my journey. However, nothing has been more important to me than what I have learned from my own soul. Most of what I have shared here has come to me from my guidance and experience. That is the way it should be for us all.

We are all Source in human form, which means we have all the knowledge of the universe within us. However, we need help to unlock that information from the vaults of our subconscious and put it into action in our lives. I am grateful to the teachers who have helped me through my trials and tribulations. Believe me, there have been many.

However, as time goes on, and I stand more in the truth of myself as Source, I am enlightened and enlivened by the strength and the power within me. I desire all humanity to feel what I feel, know what I know, and more. I am Source. You are Source. Together, we are Source.

The goal is to transcend the roller coaster of human emotions and exist in a state of eternal bliss. I remember the first time I saw the drawing below. It was 1998, and I was still in the early stages of serious spiritual study. The wave on the bottom represents the ups and downs of the human experience, and the line across the top represents the spiritual master.

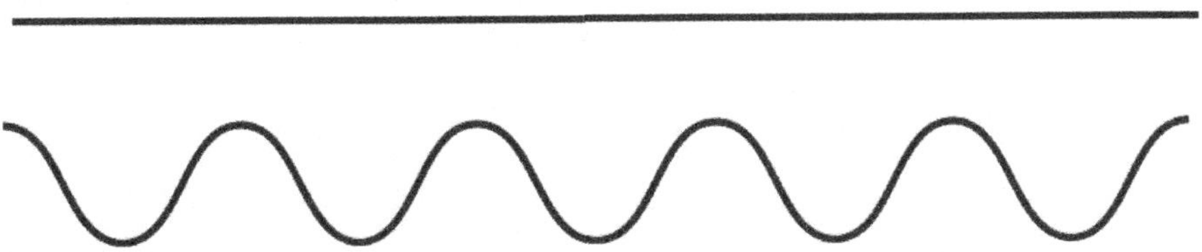

I thought this concept was ridiculous. After all, the emotional roller coaster makes us human and makes life interesting. The straight, emotionless line above seemed contrary to human growth, not to mention boring. How could we appreciate the highs if we did not also experience the lows?

Of course, over time, I understood the wisdom and the inevitability of this teaching. As we heal the lower-frequency emotions, our overall frequency has to go higher. As our overall frequency goes higher, our emotions fluctuate less and less. We find ourselves in a state of happiness and peace more often than in a state of anger and stress. Eventually, nothing remains but bliss.

Bliss is *not* boring! Bliss is our natural state and the one that reminds us of who we are as divine and sacred.

To quote one of my favorite sci-fi characters, Mr. Spock, "Live long and prosper."[33] You are life everlasting and power far beyond your limiting beliefs. Know who you are as an aspect of Source and the creator of your reality. The end of duality is yours through understanding, intention, and practice. Be bound for Ascension. Do not let anyone or anything block you from knowing the eternal bliss of oneness and all that you are.

[33] Roddenbery, Gene, *Star Trek* (1996; NBC).

Afterword

What are your plans, my wandering brother?
—*Autobiography of a Yogi* by Paramahansa Yogananda

This book has been a joy to write. I believe that every teacher who writes a book wants to share more than the pages of one volume will allow. I have written this one as a guide to understanding how we became so dense and what we will be experiencing as we move toward Ascension. The ten steps in the last chapter are ones I follow, and I feel they will help you, too.

No matter how well written, no book can take the place of sitting in class with other students, experiencing that energy, participating in conversations, and listening to a qualified teacher in the field answer questions. If you are guided to explore the Standing in the Light® process, the website listed on the next page will direct you to classes and retreats to serve your needs. If you are guided to a different course of study, get into a class, and experience all you can. If you trust your guidance, you will find yourself in the right place for you.

Just as Yogananda wandered and questioned, we must all wade through the volumes of possibilities for our evolution. Whatever you do, stay the course. Do not let yourself get sidetracked, which can happen so easily. The energies of the planet are catapulting humanity into evolution. I speak from experience when I say it is much easier to ride the waves than to be tumbled by them. As we jokingly say in Standing in the Light®, wax your surfboard and get ready for the ride. Paddle out to that perfect wave and ride it to Ascension.

https://iamstandinginthelight.com/

I love their blog!

With Gratitude

My intention is always that the people who read my writings find what they need most. I hope what you have learned here will help you as you continue to climb the staircase of Ascension no matter what path you decide to follow. As I did at the beginning of this book, I ask you to do two things.

Frist, if you have found *Awaken to Ascension* helpful to your journey, please recommend it to your friends and rate it on the site where you purchased it—or on the format of your choice such as Goodreads or Goggle. If you feel guided, take an extra minute to post a review of what you liked best to help others decide if this book might be right for them. Other people want to know what you think, and your feedback is important to me.

Leave an Amazon rating or review at Create a Review

Second, I invite you to join my mailing list. As a member, you will receive the free pdf, "7 Steps to Creating Lasting Change in Your Life: A Guide to Personal Transformation," new post notifications for my blog, and announcements about new books and specials. I try to keep it simple.

Join Marsha's Mailing List at https://marshahankins.com/mailing-list/

Share the love, and may you know yourself as Source. Namaste.

Acknowledgments

With deep gratitude, I acknowledge the following people for their contributions and support in bringing the three editions of this book into form. First, I want to thank the many teachers I have had over the years. Some of my teachers have been in body, but many have been out of body. Many have been formal teachers in classrooms, and many have been students who have taught me as they passed through my classes.

I especially thank Kris Duffy for her teachings and support as my friend and mentor. I once told her I did not know how I would have gotten so far down my path without her. She replied that I did not need her at all and came ready-made for the journey. However, I know my road would have been much longer and more laborious without her guidance and wisdom.

My deep gratitude and profound respect also go to Nancy Lee, who went line by line with me through the first edition of this book. Her insights and experience as a writer, interviewer, and psychic were a great help, and she made this project much more fun.

I am honored to have Brian Luke Seaward, Ph.D. as the author of the foreword for this book. He is doing incredible work to assist humanity in moving toward wisdom and light, and I am grateful to have his energy as part of this book.

My thanks to Rebecca Cribelli for her drawings and to Sarah Hohenberger, Nadia Mora Lara, Teresa Cribelli, and Helen Schledewitz-McGinnis, who contributed their personal stories.

I also want to thank my editors and proofreaders: Julie Hygh, Lori Rock, Ginger Withee, Vivian Anderson, Debbie Weaver, Teresa Cribelli, Myron Des Jarlais, Chris Permar, and Kendra Keene.

And, most importantly, I want to thank all who are waking up to who they are as spiritual beings. Moving from our dense beginnings on this planet to our Ascension is not easy. We have been through a great deal since we first came into the Experiment in Duality. But we will continue to expand ourselves until all humanity awakens to the truth of who we are. Ascension is our destiny because we are Source.

About the Author

The kingdom is inside you, and it is outside you.
When you know yourselves, then you will be known,
and you will understand that you are children of the living father.
—*The Gospel of Thomas*,
The Gnostic Bible: Revised and Expanded Edition, verse 3

Marsha Hankins has been a spiritual teacher and facilitator for more than 25 years. Her passion for teaching is evident as she shares her experiences of spiritual evolution with others. Marsha believes the goal of life is raising our frequency to remember who we are as aspects of Source and to be pure love. She shares her knowledge and awareness of the ascension process with understanding and compassion for our spiritual growth. She hopes her insights and techniques will help others find spiritual mastery.

Marsha teaches what she knows based on her personal experiences of healing and expansion and those of her students and clients. Her desire is to help others cross the 4th-dimensional bridge of awareness into full 5th-dimensional consciousness. She believes we all need teachers, but the final steps are up to us. The spiritual journey is about stepping into our power and trusting ourselves as Source.

Marsha is the creator of Standing in the Light®: 4th and 5th Dimensional Procedures for Experiencing Oneself as Source, My Body is My Temple: Techniques to Assist the Body in Holding More Light, and other classes to help humanity understand and experience themselves as Source. She is the author of many articles and books. Marsha is the founder of

Eminent Reiki® and ordained in the Order of Melchizedek through the Sanctuary of the Beloved.

While she is now semi-retired from teaching, Marsha cannot imagine not being of service. She still trains teachers and facilitators, teaches seminars upon request, loves public speaking, and continues to write.

Contact Marsha and read her blog on her website:
https://marshahankins.com/

Made in United States
North Haven, CT
20 July 2024

55165653R00111